LITTLE BOOK OF
EDINBURGH

Janey Fletcher

LITTLE BOOK OF
EDINBURGH

First published in the UK in 2014

© Demand Media Limited 2014

www.demand-media.co.uk

Printed and bound in Europe

ISBN 978-1-910270-78-3

Contents

Chapter 1

Capital City

Edinburgh is situated in Lothian on the south shores of the Firth of Forth. It is the second most populated city in Scotland behind Glasgow.

Since the 15th century, Edinburgh has been recognised as the capital of Scotland. After the Union of the Crowns in 1603 and the Union of Parliament in 1707, all political power was moved south to London. However, after nearly three centuries of unitary government, a devolved Scottish parliament has been sitting since 1999.

Edinburgh's economy is relatively buoyant and is traditionally centered on banking and insurance. The city now houses a wide range of businesses and is the largest financial centre in the UK after London. Indeed, many of the largest Scottish companies have their head offices in the city.

Many national institutions have also made their home in Edinburgh such as the National Museum of Scotland, the National Library of Scotland and the Scottish National Gallery along with the General Assembly of the Church of Scotland.

The city is also known internationally as a centre for education, specialising in the fields of medicine, law, sciences and engineering. There are four universities in the city and many independent schools.

Edinburgh is rich in history and has many beautiful historic buildings that include Edinburgh Castle, Holyrood Palace, and the churches of St Giles, Greyfriars and Canongate. Both of Edinburgh's Old Town and New Town are jointly listed as a UNESCO World Heritage site.

The city is also famous for its International Festival consisting of high profile theatre productions and classical music performances during August each year and includes the Edinburgh Fringe, a hotbed of ground-breaking comedy acts. Edinburgh is also known as the City of Literature, the first accolade of its kind to be awarded by UNESCO. Edinburgh is the second most popular tourist destination in the UK attracting more than one million overseas visitors a year and is second in popularity only to London. There are many historical and

ABOVE Arthurs Seat

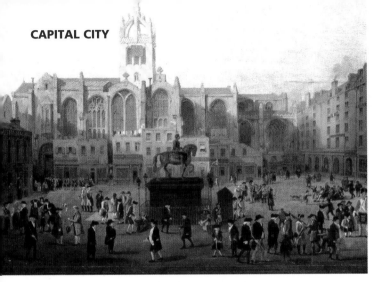

ABOVE
Parliament Close

Edinburgh was being described as the capital of Scotland. The 17th century saw a growth in the boundaries of Edinburgh although many of the houses increased in height to remain behind the city's defensive town walls. Some of these buildings were over 11 stories high and could be described as forerunners for the modern day skyscraper. Though the 18th century saw the growing importance of Edinburgh with its rising prosperity, especially in the banking business, it had a bad reputation as one of the most densely populated, overcrowded and unsanitary towns of Europe.

Towards the latter end of the century, after the Jacobite rising of 1745, Edinburgh's town council initiated many city improvements and an expansion to the north of the castle. These acts, along with the Scottish Enlightenment movement, with figures such as David Hume, James Hutton and Joseph Black lent Edinburgh a reputation for learning and its nickname "Athens of the North."

Both of the 19th and 20th centuries

cultural attractions throughout the city and its annual calendar of events make it very popular to all manners of tourists.

The name Edinburgh is said to have been of Celtic origin, derived from the Cumbran language spoken by an Iron Age tribe which the Romans called the Votadini. It is believed that the area of Edinburgh was first inhabited in the Mesolithic age c.8500 BC; however settlements from both the bronze and Iron Age were also believed to have existed on Castle Rock, Arthur's seat and in the Pentland Hills.

In the early 12th century it was King David I who founded the Royal Burgh, and by the middle of the 14th century, saw little industrialisation in Edinburgh in comparison with other great cities of Britain. Edinburgh's traditional industries such as printing, brewing and distilling did continue to grow; however, Glasgow overtook Edinburgh as Scotland's largest city in 1821.

Edinburgh Castle dominates the skyline sitting on the Castle Rock and has been at the forefront of many historical conflicts throughout its history. Sadly, many of the mediaeval defences have been destroyed by artillery bombardment; however St Margaret's Chapel is a notable exception and is regarded by many as the oldest building in Edinburgh, dating back from the early 12th century.

Within the castle are the Scottish Crown Jewels, known as the Honours of Scotland, which date from the 15th and 16th centuries and are reputed to be the oldest set of Crown Jewels in the British Isles. They consist of the Crown, the Sceptre and the Sword of State, all three elements also appearing on the crest of the royal coat of arms for Scotland.

Edinburgh Castle is also the site of the Scottish National War Memorial and incorporates the National War Museum of Scotland. Even though its presence is ceremonial and largely administrative, the British Army is still responsible for some parts of Edinburgh Castle. Within the castle are several regimental museums.

BELOW St Giles Cathedral Interior

CLIMATE DATA FOR EDINBURGH (Royal Botanic Gardens)

Month	Jan	Feb	Mar	Apr	May	Jun	Jul	Aug	Sep	Oct	Nov	Dec	Year
Record high °C	15.0	15.2	20.0	22.8	29.0	27.8	30.0	31.4	26.7	24.4	17.3	15.4	31.4
(°F)	(59)	(59.4)	(68)	(73)	(84.2)	(82)	(86)	(88.5)	(80.1)	(75.9)	(63.1)	(59.7)	(88.5)
Average high °C (°F)	7.0	7.5	9.5	11.8	14.7	17.2	19.1	18.9	16.5	13.1	9.6	7.0	12.66
	(44.6)	(45.5)	(49.1)	(53.2)	(58.5)	(63)	(66.4)	(66)	(61.7)	(55.6)	(49.3)	(44.6)	(54.79)
Average low °C (°F)	1.4	1.5	2.8	4.3	6.8	9.7	11.5	11.4	9.4	6.5	3.7	1.3	5.86
	(34.5)	(34.7)	(37)	(39.7)	(44.2)	(49.5)	(52.7)	(52.5)	(48.9)	(43.7)	(38.7)	(34.3)	(42.53)
Record low °C	−15.5	−11.7	−11.1	−6.1	−2.4	1.1	4.4	2.2	−1.1	−3.7	−8.3	−11.5	−15.5
(°F)	(4.1)	(10.9)	(12)	(21)	(27.7)	(34)	(39.9)	(36)	(30)	(25.3)	(17.1)	(11.3)	(4.1)
Precipitation mm (inches)	67.5	47.0	51.7	40.5	48.9	61.3	65.0	60.2	63.7	75.6	62.1	60.8	704.3
	(2.657)	(1.85)	(2.035)	(1.594)	(1.925)	(2.413)	(2.559)	(2.37)	(2.508)	(2.976)	(2.445)	(2.394)	(27.726)
Avg. rainy days	12.5	9.4	9.9	8.8	9.6	9.6	9.5	9.7	10.2	12.4	11.2	11.4	124.2
Mean monthly sunshine hours	53.5	78.5	114.8	144.6	188.4	165.9	172.2	161.5	128.8	101.2	71.0	46.2	1,426.6

Source: Met Office

More than 1.2 million visitors tour Edinburgh Castle, making it Scotland's most visited paid tourist attraction in the care of Historic Scotland.

Within Edinburgh city are more than 4500 listed buildings, this is pro-rata a higher proportion in relation to area than in any other city within the UK.

Despite being in northerly latitude, Edinburgh has a temperate maritime climate which is relatively mild. It is rare for winter daytime temperatures to fall below freezing. Even though Edinburgh sits on similar latitude to Moscow, its climate is much milder.

During the summer, temperatures rarely exceed 22°C, with the highest ever temperature being recorded in August 1975 at 31°C. The lowest temperature to have been recorded in recent years was in December 2010, a chilly -14.6°C!

Edinburgh has been called the 'windy city' as it sits between the coast and the surrounding hills with the prevailing wind coming from the south west bringing warm and unstable air from the North Atlantic current.

Peculiar to the city can be a persistent coastal fog which is called a 'haar', which usually occurs when the winds are from an easterly direction.

The city centre is two and a half miles

Southwest from the shoreline of Leith, within Scotland's Central Belt, lying on the southern shores of the Firth of Forth. Edinburgh itself consists of seven hills, the most famous being, of course, Castle Rock.

To the south and west of Edinburgh is the river called the Water of Leith, which empties into the Firth of Forth at Leith. In 1957, the outer surrounds of Edinburgh was designated a green belt area, the objective being to prevent outward expansion of the city and urban sprawl. Although expansion has been strictly controlled, there have been exceptions to the rule, such as Edinburgh airport and the Royal Highland Showground.

When the railways were introduced into Edinburgh in the 1840s, it became more imperative to improve the dilapidated and overcrowded slum areas with their unacceptably high mortality rates. It was William Chambers, the Lord Provost of Edinburgh, who initiated the transformation in the old town area, more improvements being carried out by Patrick Geddes later in the 20th century.

During the 1990s the financial district of Edinburgh grew towards the west side of the castle. Originally a run down 19th century industrial suburb, this has now become the second largest financial and administrative centre in the UK and

CAPITAL CITY

RIGHT Location of Edinburgh within Scotland

BELOW View of Edinburgh from Blackford Hill

includes Edinburgh's International Conference Centre.

The corporate headquarters of Johnston Press, which own The Scotsman, are based in Edinburgh; this national newspaper is the only one to be published in the city. However the Edinburgh Evening News is also published every day except on Sunday.

Two commercial radio stations are housed in Edinburgh; Forth 1 plays mainstream chart music, whilst Forth 2 plays more classical music. Both Capital Radio Scotland and Real Radio Scotland have transmitters in Edinburgh; Radio Scotland and the Gaelic language BBC radio service are also broadcast in the city.

Television is broadcast to Edinburgh from the Craig Kelly transmitting station, which can be found in Fife on the opposite side of the Firth of Forth.

Edinburgh boasts many museums and libraries including the National Museum of Scotland; the National Library of Scotland; the National War

Museum of Scotland; the Museum of Edinburgh; Surgeons Hall Museum; and the Museum of Childhood.

The second largest paid tourist attraction in Scotland is Edinburgh Zoo, which covers 33 hectares on Corstorphine Hill, and is famous for being the current home to two giant pandas on loan from the People's Republic of China.

There are five National Galleries of Art in Edinburgh with many smaller art galleries also well established in the city. Linked to the Royal Scottish Academy is the National Gallery of Scotland which is to be found on the Mound in Edinburgh, where the National Collection is housed.

The gallery is also linked with the Royal Scottish Academy, holding regular major painting exhibitions. The Scottish National Gallery of Modern Art displays many contemporary collections and can be found at Belford. On Queen Street sits the Scottish National Portrait Gallery, displaying many famous portraits and photography.

The Fruit Market Gallery in Edinburgh features works by British and international artists both those with international reputations and emerging exciting young talents.

Shoppers are well catered for in Edinburgh. Within the city, the main shopping area is Princes Street dotted with souvenir shops and chain stores. The more upmarket and independent stores can be found on George Street to the north of Princes Street.

At Multrees Walk, next to St James's Centre are some rather more exclusive

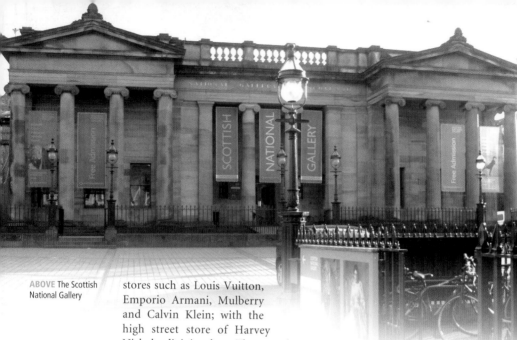

stores such as Louis Vuitton, Emporio Armani, Mulberry and Calvin Klein; with the high street store of Harvey Nichols adjoining them. There are also many retail parks situated out of the city centre of Edinburgh.

The local council (one of 32 in Scotland) deals with all civic administration including housing, planning, local transport, economic development and regeneration within Edinburgh.

Five members of parliament represent Edinburgh in the House of Commons. Each constituency - Edinburgh North and Leith; Edinburgh East; Edinburgh South; Edinburgh South West; and Edinburgh West - elect one member by the first past the post system.

Edinburgh's airport handles more than nine million passengers a year and is Scotland's biggest and busiest airport. With this in mind, future plans are being made to expand both the airfield and the terminal building with the introduction of a second runway.

The bus service in Edinburgh is run by Lothian Buses who operate not only the city's normal travel links but also

handle the public tour buses, a night bus service and the airport bus link. More than 109 million passengers travelled on these buses in 2010.

Edinburgh is often remembered for its trams but has been without a tram system since November 1956. Following parliamentary approval construction began on a new Edinburgh tram line in early 2008. The first stage was due to be completed by July 2011 but lengthy contractual disputes have delayed the opening; although trams were due to begin operating by the middle of 2014.

Waverly, Edinburgh's railway station is the fifth busiest station outside London and the UK's second largest station in terms of platforms. Most trains arriving from London's Kings Cross station end at Waverly which connects to many stations throughout Scotland.

Edinburgh has been at the forefront of the park and ride scheme and now has six such sites on the outer rim of the city.

Chapter 2

The Economy

Edinburgh is the powerhouse of the Scottish economy and also has huge importance in the wider UK economy.

Edinburgh has been consistently one of the most prosperous parts of the country and has the strongest economy of any city in the UK outside London.

The population of Edinburgh now exceeds 475,000. Employment is high - with nearly three quarters of the population in work - while the city has the second highest gross value added (GVA) per resident. The average gross annual earnings per resident are £27,800, which is second only to London.

Top employers in the city include NHS Lithium; City of Edinburgh Council; the University of Edinburgh; the Royal Bank of Scotland group; Lloyds Banking Group and Standard Life.

For over 300 years, Edinburgh has been an important centre of banking. It is the second largest financial centre in the UK and fourth in Europe.

Both the Royal Bank of Scotland and the Lloyds Banking Group have their headquarters in the city of Edinburgh; the RBS now being the fifth largest in the world.

It is famous for some of the biggest banking takeovers in British history; they have now acquired such banks as the National Westminster Bank, Ulster Bank, Direct Line and Coutts. Other well-known banks to keep their headquarters in Edinburgh are Virgin Money and Tesco Bank.

Not only strong in banking, Edinburgh also houses many large insurance

companies such as Standard Life and Scottish Widows. The latter, founded in 1815, has a workforce of around 3500 people and in June 2013 was managing £145.79 billion worth of funds.

Most of the banking, finance and legal professions have traditionally been in the city centre and the New Town. However, many have now relocated to the west of the city in The Exchange business district which houses such companies as Scottish Widows, Standard Life, the Clydesdale Bank and Bailley Gifford.

Located near to Edinburgh Airport is Edinburgh Park, which is one of the largest business parks in the UK. It opened in 1992 with a large out-of-town shopping development and is conveniently located to major routes such as the A8, the M8 and the A720 City bypass. It also has its own railway station.

Other large banking organisations

THE ECONOMY

such as HSBC, Royal bank, JP Morgan, BT, Fujitsu and Lloyds banking group have all got large offices in Edinburgh Park. More than 20,000 people work in this western outskirt of the city.

There is perhaps no region more associated with the history of brewing in Scotland than that of Edinburgh and its environs. The brewing industry certainly contributed to Edinburgh's earned moniker of 'Auld Reekie' so named due to all the smoke produced by coal and wood burning furnaces and boilers.

This is evidenced by the fact that at the turn of the 19th to 20th centuries, Edinburgh had no less than 35 breweries churning out this smoke from its maltings and brew houses. This haze may not have been so noticeable were it not for the denseness of the buildings and population in such proximity.

Two of Scotland's largest, most historic and most successful brewing firms were established in Edinburgh. William Younger started brewing in Leith around the year 1749, and went on to launch the Abbey and Holyrood Breweries. William McEwan founded his famous Fountain Brewery in the year 1856 and also became hugely successful.

Long after their founders were gone, the two breweries eventually merged and ultimately became Scottish & Newcastle. Sadly, with the closing of the Fountain Brewery in the late 1990's, nothing is left of these once great breweries.

Many other brewers were very successful in and around Edinburgh over the years as well. Names such as Ushers, Drybrough, John Jeffrey, T. & J. Bernard, Lorimer & Clark and Steel Coulson & Co. all ran very successful and long lived breweries in Edinburgh throughout most of the 19th and 20th centuries.

Nearby, Mark Binnie & Co. ran the Nungate Brewery in Haddington for many years as did John Fowler in Prestonpans. The Belhaven Brewery in Dunbar dates back as far as 1719 and was managed for much of its life under Dudgeon & Co. It remains as Scotland's oldest established brewery still in operation although England's Greene King now owns it.

Although many of these famous and historic brewers are now long gone, these great brewing traditions live on at the Caledonian Brewery (established by Lorimer & Clark in 1869) in Edinburgh.

Also in the Edinburgh environs are Stewart Brewing (est. 2004), Knops Beer Company (2010) and the Eclipse Brewery (2012). Innis & Gunn also have offices in Edinburgh but beer is brewed under contract.

Near to but outside of Edinburgh are Alechemy Brewing (2012) at Livingston; Demon Brew (2011) at the Gothenburg pub in Prestonpans; and the Kinneil Brew Hoose (2011) at Bo'ness. And finally, well known the world over, Belhaven Brewery (dating back to 1719) continues to brew at Dunbar.

Leith lies to the north of the city of Edinburgh at the mouth of the Water of Leith and has long been regarded as Edinburgh's principal port, on the south shore of the Firth of Forth.

It officially became Edinburgh's port in 1329 when Robert I transferred control to the magistrates and citizens of Edinburgh and remains a busy port to this day, handling more than 1.5 million tonnes of cargo a year.

Leith has been a pioneering industrial centre for many centuries. Notably, the Leith Glassworks has stood on Baltic Street from 1746 specialising in producing wine

THE ECONOMY

BELOW The
Caledonian Brewery

bottles, mainly for export to France and Spain. In 1770, production was a staggering one million bottles per week.

The Leith pattern bottle is the parallel-sided, round-shouldered, narrow neck bottle which now dominates the wine industry. Soon after 1770, the company branched into lead crystal glass, mainly for chandeliers. This was under a new company by the name of the Edinburgh Crystal Company which stood on the same site in Leith.

Whisky production has always played a major part in Edinburgh's economy. The Sanderson's distillery was based in Leith from 1863, and is famous for its Vat 69 and Mountain Dew scotch blends. The distillery became a limited company in 1896 and was known as William Sanderson & Son Limited. Production was moved from Leith to South Queensferry in 1969.

LEFT The Younger's Abbey Brewery in Canongate

The storage of wine and whisky in Leith dates from at least the early 16th century, when it used to be connected with the vaults on Henderson Street. During its peak, there were around 100 warehouses storing wine and brandy; however, in the late 1880s wine harvest in Europe collapsed, most of these were converted to whisky storage.

More than 85 bonded warehouses used to stand in Leith in the 1960s which jointly matured around 90% of all Scotch whisky. One of the largest, Crabbies on Great Junction Street, stored whisky for some of the foremost whisky distilleries such as Lagavulin, Talisker and Laphroaig.

Although now sadly no longer an important industry, shipbuilding on the Water of Leith was a large source of income to the economy. However, as vessels started to increase in size, Leith's shallow port could not sustain new growth, so it began to specialise in odd ship types such as tugs, hotel ships and cable-layers.

Whilst the most notable large shipyard Henry Robb's, closed around 1981, this was technically outlived by a very small ship-builder, Sherrif Brae (run by the Scottish Co-operative Society) which closed in 1988.

Famous ships to be built in Leith include SS Sirius, one of the first steam-ships to cross the Atlantic; and SS Copenhagen one of the largest rigged ships ever built. Robb's yard also made a great contribution to the Royal Navy and Merchant Navy during the Second World War, building 42 vessels for the Royal Navy, 14 merchant ships, and refitted and repaired nearly 3,000 ships for the Royal Navy and Merchant Navy. A new ship was launched every six weeks on average and a ship repaired every day of this long and bloody conflict.

One of Scotland's largest lead works stood on the corner of Mitchell Street and Constitution Street in Leith. Founded in around 1760, the operational part worked until the 1970s, while the empty buildings stood on the site until the late 1980s.

The offices on Constitution Street still survive. The company specialised in lead pipes for water supply and lead drainpipes. They also produced lead sheet for roofing and lead shot for weapons.

The mainstay of Leith for centuries was the rather ghastly whaling industry. This was originally in the local waters but was then expanded to travel to both Icelandic

TOP 10 TOURIST ATTRACTIONS IN EDINBURGH, 2012	
Tourist attraction	**Number of visitors**
National Museum of Scotland	1,893,500
Edinburgh Castle	1,230,200
Scottish National Gallery	961,300
St Giles' Cathedral	904,400
Edinburgh Zoo	810,900
Royal Botanic Garden Edinburgh	704,600
Edinburgh Bus Tours	511,400
National War Museum	492,700
Scottish Parliament Visitor Centre	345,100
Our Dynamic Earth	331,800
Scottish National Portrait Gallery	328,000
Scottish National Gallery of Modern Art	314,800
Royal Yacht Britannia	300,700
Scottish Whisky Heritage Centre	270,600
Museum of Childhood	237,500
Source: Moffat Centre Visitor Attraction Monitor 2012	

and Antarctic waters. The last whale in the Firth of Forth was caught in 1834.

The company moved from Leith to Fettes around 1980 and then left Edinburgh altogether in the mid-1990s. The founder of the main whaling company, Christian Salvesen was buried in Rosebank Cemetery. Interestingly, the whale ships from Leith brought the very first penguins to Edinburgh Zoo around 1900.

Although Glasgow has the most significant retail sector of Scotland,

THE ECONOMY

Edinburgh has many large out-of-town shopping developments including the Gyle development completed in 1993 and the Fort Kinnaird shopping located in the east of the city.

The city centre has seen a decline similar to other sized cities, in particular, Princes Street. However attempts to lure the shoppers back into the city centre have been made including new top brand department stores located on George Street and St Andrew Square, there are also plans afoot to redevelop Princes Street and the St James Centre.

It is estimated that tourism is worth over £1.6 billion to Edinburgh city's economy. Tourism supports 30,000 jobs in the city with the National Museum of Scotland being the most popular tourist destination. The numbers grow substantially every year and this has been assisted by the improvement in direct rail links and the growth of Edinburgh airport.

Celebrations such as the Edinburgh Festival and the Hogmanay street parties in the New Year also bring in substantial numbers of tourists.

TOP EMPLOYMENT SECTORS, CITY OF EDINBURGH	
Sector	**Number of employees**
Human health and social work	45,300
Wholesale, retail and repair	36,400
Financial Services	34,600
Education	29,200
Accommodation and food services	26,800
Professional, scientific and technical activities	27,100
Administrative and support services activities	21,000
Public administration, defence and social security	18,700
Information and communication	12,400
Transportation and storage	10,200
Arts, entertainment and recreation	10,000
Construction	9,000
Manufacturing	7,300
Other service activities	5,500
Primary industries and utilities	3,200
Real Estate	5,200
Source: Edinburgh by Numbers 2013/14	

Chapter 3

Festivals

During the month of August, Edinburgh hosts many artistic and cultural festivals. The original and largest is the Edinburgh International Festival and the Edinburgh Festival Fringe. In fact, the Edinburgh Festival Fringe is now larger than any other similar event held globally.

The Edinburgh International Festival is held over three weeks running from the middle of August and is one of the most important cultural celebrations in the world. Performers take part by invitation only from the Festival Director, with many top class international musicians, actors and dancers on the roster.

Conceived after the Second World War, the idea behind the festival was to enrich the cultural life of Scotland, Britain and Europe. The founders of the Festival included Rudolph Bing, General Manager of the Glyndebourne Opera Festival; Henry Hollywood, Head

of the British Council in Scotland; Sydney Newman Reid, Professor of Music at Edinburgh University; and the Lord Provost, Sir John Falconer.

These founders had a vision that the festival should enliven and enrich the cultural life of Europe. They believed profoundly that a world-class cultural event would bring together people and artists from around the globe, generating significant cultural, social and economic benefits for both Edinburgh and Scotland.

Many other festivals have grown up around the International Festival, most notably the Edinburgh Festival Fringe, the Military Tattoo and Book, Jazz and Mela Festivals. These other events have now been expanded into other times of the year and include the Hogmanay Festival, and the Science and Children's Festivals.

ABOVE The view of the Old Town from Princes Street during the International Festival

LEFT Flyers for Fringe performances covering a phone box

The Edinburgh International Festival now has a permanent home in the Hub, formerly the Highland Tolbooth featuring Edinburgh's most prominent spire which can be seen over the Royal Mile.

The Edinburgh Festival Fringe is now the largest arts festival in the world, with more than 2500 performances taking place in over 250 venues with performers from more than 47 countries. The event takes place in August and was initiated in 1947 as an alternative to the Edinburgh International Festival.

The Edinburgh Festival Fringe includes many performing arts, in particular theatrical and comedy although music and dance are also very much part of the productions. As there is no selec-

The Edinburgh Festival fringe has helped launch the careers of many famous writers and performers including Alan Bennett, Dudley Moore, Peter Cook and Jonathan Miller who in the

LEFT TOP Street Performances during the Edinburgh Fringe Festival

LEFT BOTTOM Tight rope walking during the Edinburgh Fringe Festival

tion committee, any type of performer may enter which has led to many experimental works included in the festival.

In the past, theatre had been the largest genre in terms of number of shows, but recently this has been overtaken by comedy which has grown hugely in the last 20 years.

early 1960s first staged Beyond the Fringe at the Royal Lyceum Theatre.

Playwright Tom Stoppard first staged 'Rosencrantz and Guildenstern Are Dead' at the festival in 1966.

In recent years, established stars came back to perform and try out new routines

ABOVE LEFT Writers Ian Rankin and Ruth Rendall at Edinburgh's Book Festival

ABOVE RIGHT Taking a break during Edinburgh's Book Festival

ABOVE Edinburgh
Castle as the
backdrop to the
Tattoo

RIGHT Fireworks
over the Royal
Military Tattoo

ternational Book Festival which is housed in Charlotte Square and is the largest festival of its kind in the world. The Festival was originally conceived in 1983 and hosts many cultural and political talks and debates as well a popular children's events programme.

Along with the Edinburgh International Festival and the Edinburgh Fringe, the Edinburgh International Book Festival takes place in August.

Many famous writers have been invited to the festival including Margaret Atwood, Alan Bennett, Sebastian Faulks, Germaine Greer, Harold Pinter, Ian Rankin, JK Rowling, Salman Rushdie and Alexander McCall Smith to name but a few.

The Royal Edinburgh Military Tattoo is an annual event in August and part of the wider Edinburgh Festival. The military tattoos are performed by British Armed Forces, Commonwealth and international military bands and take place on the esplanade of Edinburgh Castle.

The derivation of the word tattoo comes from 'to tap toe'. It was in Flanders where the British Army first encountered such a practice during the War of the Austrian Succession.

although Ricky Gervais, writer and star of 'The Office', was accused of greed when he used the Military Tattoo's 6000-seat venue for a one-off performance of his stand-up show: his answer to this was to donate to the profits of the show to the MacMillan Cancer Support charity.

Over the years there has also been criticism over the quality of shows at the Fringe. Michael Dale, fringe administrator, answered these criticisms by pointing out that quality was not of paramount importance: the point being that the fringe was created to provide a forum for ideas and achievements unique in the UK and the world.

The city also hosts the Edinburgh In-

The tattoo became a signal, and was played by each regiment's Corps of Drums or Pipes every night as a signal to the local tavern owners to stop serving ale, ensuring that the soldiers would return to their lodgings. In modern day practice, the tattoo was used to describe the last duty call of the day and also became the ceremonial form for evening entertainment.

The first tattoo in Edinburgh was held in 1949 at the Princes Street Gardens and was called "Something about a Soldier"; while the 'official' Edinburgh military Tattoo was initiated in 1950, drawing some 6000 spectators to the Edinburgh Castle esplanade.

Nowadays, more than 217,000 people come to watch the live tattoo, with the seats having been sold out every year for the last decade. Only 30% of the audience is Scottish, 35% coming from the rest of the United Kingdom and the remainder are visitors from overseas.

Throughout August, the tattoo is performed every weekday evening and twice on Saturdays and has never been cancelled for bad weather. On the last Saturday night performance, there is a spectacular fireworks display and a 'son et lumiere' which highlights the facade of the castle.

From 2004 onwards, the Edinburgh Military Tattoo holds free performances at the original Ross Bandstand in the Princes Street Gardens; it has also recently been giving free performances in Glasgow.

For the 50th anniversary celebrations of the Edinburgh Tattoo, the performance was taken overseas to New Zealand in 2000. It was also performed in the Sydney Football Stadium in Australia to celebrate the 60th anniversary of the Tattoo.

More than 100 million people watch the Edinburgh Military Tattoo worldwide, as the BBC televises it in over 30 countries. The late Tom Fleming had commentated on the Tattoo from 1966 to 2008, however it is now Bill Paterson who provides the commentary.

The Tattoo is thought to generate more than £88 million annually for Edinburgh's economy and is run for charitable causes, with more than £5 million being donated to both military and civilian charities.

The flavour of the Edinburgh Military Tattoo has been deliberately kept international in order to entertain a huge cosmopolitan audience. It has the unique ability to draw thousands of people together to celebrate both music and entertainment with spectacular pomp and ceremony.

Hogmanay is the Scottish word for the last day of the year. It is the Scottish celebration of the New Year and usually starts through the night until the morning of New Years Day.

Edinburgh's Hogmanay has now become one of the biggest and best New Year celebrations throughout the world. On the night of 31st December there is a spectacular torchlight procession where thousands of torch carriers create a living river of fire running from the historic Royal Mile to the son et lumière and the fireworks finale which are held on Calton Hill.

On the evening of Hogmanay itself, more than 80,000 people gather to party in Princes Street with the spectacular illuminated backdrop of Edinburgh Castle. A huge concert - featuring live music and entertainment, DJs, giant screens, outdoor bars – ends with the midnight Hogmanay fireworks held on Edinburgh Castle's ramparts.

The early New Year morning often sees many partygoers plunging into the freezing River Forth at South Queensferry; this is called the Loony Dook, with many dressing up in fancy dress for the occasion.

History

The earliest known human habitation in the Edinburgh area was at Cramond where evidence has been found of a Mesolithic site dated to c.8500 BC.

Traces of later Bronze Age and Iron Age settlements have been found on Castle Rock, Arthur's Seat, Craiglockhart Hill and the Pentland Hills.

The culture of these early inhabitants bears similarities with the Celtic cultures of the Iron Age found at Hallstatt and La Tene in central Europe.

When the Romans arrived in Lothian towards the end of the 1st century AD, they discovered a Celtic Brythonic tribe whose name they recorded as the Votadini.

At some point before the 7th century AD, the Gododdin, presumed descendants of the Votadini, built a hill fort known as Din Eidyn or Etin, almost certainly somewhere within the bounds of modern Edinburgh.

Although the exact location of the hill fort has not been identified, it seems more than likely they would have chosen the commanding position of the Castle Rock, or Arthur's Seat or the Calton Hill.

During the time of the Gododdin, the territory of Lothian came into existence, with Edinburgh as its main stronghold. Around the year 600, Welsh tradition records that Mynyddog Mwynfawr, the Brythonic ruler of the kingdom of Gododdin, assembled a force within the vicinity of Edinburgh to oppose Germanic settlers to the south. This force was decisively defeated by the Angles at the Battle of Catraeth (probably Catterick).

NORTHUMBRIAN EDINBURGH
(7th to 10th centuries)

The Angles of the Kingdom of Bernicia had a significant influence on what would be successively Bernicia, Northumbria and finally south east Scotland, notably from AD 638 when it appears that the Gododdin stronghold was besieged by forces loyal to King Oswald of Northumbria.

Whether or not this battle marked the precise passing of control over the hill fort of Etin from the Brythonic Celts to the Northumbrians, it was around this time that the Edinburgh region came under Northumbrian rule.

In the following years the Angles extended their influence west and north of Edinburgh but following their defeat at the Battle of Nechtansmere in 685 Edinburgh may have come to mark the north west extremity of the Angles' kingdom.

Though not exclusive, Anglian influence predominated for the following three centuries with Edinburgh as a frontier stronghold. During this period Edinburgh became a place where the Northumbrian dialect of Old English was spoken and its name acquired the Old English suffix, "-burh".

While history records little about Northumbrian Edinburgh, the English chronicler Symeon of Durham, writing in c. AD 1130 and copying from earlier texts, mentioned a church at Edwinesburch in AD 854 which came under the authority of the Bishop of Lindisfarne.

It has been inferred from this report that there was therefore an established settlement by the middle of the ninth century. It is possible that this church was a forerunner of what was later to become St Giles' Cathedral. Traditionally and less certainly, Saint Cuthbert is said to have preached the gospel around the castle rock in the second half of the seventh century.

The development of a fortress on the Castle Rock is shrouded in uncertainty. It has been suggested that the Northumbrians established a stronghold in the seventh century, but the archaeological and historical evidence is scant, except for indications that by the middle of the 10th century there was some form of noble residence on the site.

In the late ninth century the Danelaw, centered on York, was established in the wake of Viking raids on Britain. The northern part of Northumbria was cut off from the rest of England by the Old Norse-speaking Danes, significantly weakening what remained of the kingdom.

During the 10th century its northernmost part, which had retained its Brythonic name Lothian, came under the sway of the Kingdom of Scotland. In 934 the Annals of Clonmacnoise record that the English king Æthelstan ravaged Scotland to Edinburgh but that he was forced to depart without any great victory.

The Chronicle of the Kings of Alba records that "oppidum Eden", usually identified as Edinburgh, "was evacuated, and abandoned to the Scots until the present day." This has been read as indicating that Lothian was ceded to the Scottish king Indulf who reigned from AD 954 to 962. Thereafter Edinburgh generally remained under the jurisdiction of the Scots.

In AD 973 the English King Edgar the Peaceful formally granted Lothian to Kenneth II, King of Scots. The historian Marjorie Anderson holds that this was the key event in assuring Scottish rule over Lothian.

By the early 11th century the Scottish hold over the area was secured when Malcolm II ended the Northumbrian threat by his victory at the battle of Carham in 1018. While Malcolm Canmore

(1058-1093) kept his court and residence at Dunfermline, north of the Forth, he began spending more time at Edinburgh where he built a chapel for his wife Margaret to carry out her devotions.

St. Margaret's Chapel within Edinburgh Castle has been traditionally regarded as Edinburgh's oldest extant building, though most scholars now believe that in its surviving form it was more likely built by Margaret's youngest son David I in his mother's memory.

In the 12th century (c.1130), King David I, established the town of Edinburgh as one of Scotland's earliest royal burghs, protected by his royal fortress, on the slope below the castle rock.

Merchants were allocated strips of land known as "tofts", ranged along both sides of a long market street, on condition that they built a house on their land within a year and a day.

Each toft stretched back from the street to a perimeter dyke and formed

a private close (from Old French clos), meaning an enclosed yard. A separate, contiguous burgh of regality held by the Abbey of Holyrood developed to the east as the burgh of Canongate.

Edinburgh was largely in English hands from 1291 to 1314 and from 1333 to 1341, during the Wars of Scottish Independence.

After the loss of Scotland's main trading port Berwick to English occupation in the 1330s, the bulk of the kingdom's profitable export trade in skins, hides, and most notably wool was routed through Edinburgh and its port of Leith.

By the middle of the 14th century, in the reign of David II, the French chronicler Froissart described the town of around 400 dwellings as "the Paris of Scotland" (c.1365). The Scottish king James II (1437-60) was "born, crowned, married and buried in the Abbey of Holyrood", and James III (1451–88) described Edinburgh in one of his charters as "the principal burgh of our kingdom."

By the reign of James V (1512–42) Edinburgh's assessment for taxation sometimes equalled the combined figures for the next three burghs in the kingdom; its proportion of total burgh taxation amounting to a fifth or a quarter and its total customs to a half or more.

Despite wholesale destruction reported by contemporaries at the time of the Hertford Raid in 1544, the town slowly recovered with its population of merchant burgesses and craftsmen continuing to serve the needs of the royal court and nobility.

Incorporated trades were cordiners (shoemakers), hatmakers, websters (weavers), hammermen (smiths and lorimers, i.e. leather workers), skinners, fleshers (butchers), coopers, wrights, masons, waulkers (fullers), tailors, barber-surgeons, baxters (bakers), and candlemakers. With the rise of taxes imposed by the burgh, some of these crafts relocated to suburbs beyond the town's boundary in the 16th and 17th centuries.

In 1560, at a time when Scotland's total population was an estimated one million people, Edinburgh's population reached 12,000, with another 4,000 in separate jurisdictions such as Canongate and the port of Leith.

A parish census in 1592 recorded 8003 adults spread evenly south and north of the High Street; 45 per cent of the employed being domestic servants in the households of the legal and merchant professions or in town houses of the landed class. Despite periodic outbreaks of plague with high death rates, most notably in 1568, 1584–88 and 1645, the population continued to grow steadily.

The town played a central role in events leading to the establishment of

LEFT Portrait of James II of Scotland

BELOW Portrait of Mary, Queen of Scots

BELOW Portrait of King James VI of Scotland

Protestantism in the mid-16th century Scottish Reformation. During her brief reign the Catholic Mary, Queen of Scots, who returned to Scotland from France in 1561, suffered from the deep discord that had been sown prior to her arrival.

Protestant nobles and churchmen fearing that her personal faith and claim to the English throne, if successful, might lead eventually to a return to Catholicism remained implacably hostile to her rule. Although initially welcomed by the general population, the tragic chain of events that unfolded during her residence at Holyrood Palace, including the murders of her secretary David Rizzio and consort Henry Darnley, reached a crisis point which resulted in her forced abdication in 1567.

Through his preaching at St. Giles calling for her execution as an adulteress and murderess the town's Protestant minister John Knox inflamed popular opinion against Mary. After her arrest at Carberry she was detained briefly in the town provost's house on the present-day site of the Edinburgh City Chambers before being incarcerated in Loch Leven Castle.

The civil war that followed her escape from imprisonment, defeat at Langside and flight to England ended with the final surrender of her remaining loyal supporters in the "Lang Siege" of Edinburgh Castle in 1573.

The internal religious division within

Scottish Protestantism, between Presbyterians and Episcopalians, continued into the 17th century, culminating in the Wars of the Covenant and the Wars of the Three Kingdoms, during which Edinburgh, as the seat of the Scottish Parliament with its Kirk-dominated Committee of Estates, figured prominently.

The eventual triumph of Presbyterianism in 1689 determined the settled form of the Church of Scotland and resulted in the imposition of a Presbyterian orthodoxy over most of the country and its people.

UNION OF THE CROWNS TO PARLIAMENTARY UNION (17th century)

In 1603 King James VI of Scotland succeeded to the English throne, uniting the monarchies of Scotland and England in a regal union known as the Union of the Crowns. In all other respects Scotland remained a separate kingdom retaining the Parliament of Scotland in Edinburgh.

King James VI moved to London where he held court, relying on a Privy Council to affect his rule in Scotland. Despite promising to return to his northern kingdom every three years, he returned only once, in 1617.

In the period 1550 to 1650, Edinburgh's town council was controlled by merchants despite efforts by the king's agents to manipulate it. The most important factors in obtaining the office were social status, followed by wealth; a person's religion made relatively little difference. More than three quarters of men at the time inherited burgess status from their father or their father-in-law.

Stiff Presbyterian opposition to King Charles I's attempt to introduce Anglican forms of worship and church governance in the Church of Scotland culminated in the Bishops' Wars of 1639 and 1640, the initial conflicts in the civil war period.

In 1650, following Scottish support for the restoration of Charles Stuart to the throne of England, Edinburgh was occupied by the Commonwealth forces of Oliver Cromwell who went on to inflict a final defeat on the Scots at the Battle of Worcester.

In the 17th century, Edinburgh was still enclosed within the 140 acres of its "ancient royalty" by the defensive Flodden and Telfer Walls, built mainly in the 16th century as protection against possible English invasion.

Due to the restricted land area avail-

able for development, houses increased in height to accommodate a growing population. Buildings of 11 stories were common; some, according to contemporary travellers' accounts, even taller, as high as 14 or even 15 stories.

These were often described by later commentators as precursors of the modern day high-rise apartment block.

Most of these old structures were later replaced by the predominantly Victorian buildings of the Old Town.

In 1706 and 1707, the Acts of Union were passed by the Parliaments of England and Scotland uniting the two kingdoms into the Kingdom of Great Britain. As a consequence, the Parliament of Scotland merged with the

Parliament of England to form the Parliament of Great Britain, which sat only in London. The Union was opposed by many Scots at the time, resulting in riots within the city.

By the first half of the 18th century, rising prosperity was evidenced by the growth of the Bank of Scotland, Royal Bank of Scotland and British Linen Bank, all based in the city. However Edinburgh was one of the most densely populated, overcrowded and insanitary towns in the whole of Europe.

Daniel Defoe's remark was typical of many English visitors, "... though many cities have more people in them, yet, I believe, this may be said with truth, that in no city in the world do so many people live in so little room as at Edinburgh".

A striking characteristic of Edinburgh society in the 18th century, often remarked upon by visitors, was the close proximity and social interaction of the various social classes. Tradesmen and professionals shared the same buildings.

The populace dwelt in the flats of the lofty houses in wynds or facing the High Street and reached their various lodgings by the steep and narrow 'scale' staircases (stair-towers) which were really upright streets.

In the same building lived families of all grades and classes - the sweep and caddie in the cellars; poor mechanics in the garrets; while in the intermediate stories might live a noble, a lord of session, a doctor or city minister, a dowager countess, or writer; higher up, over their heads, lived shopkeepers, dancing masters or clerks.

One historian has ventured to suggest that Edinburgh's living arrangements may themselves have played a part in engendering the spirit of social inquiry associated with the thinkers of the Scottish Enlightenment: "Its tall lands (tenements) housed a cross-section of the entire society, nobles, judges and caddies rubbing shoulders with each other on the common stair. A man of inquiring mind could not live in old Edinburgh without becoming a sociologist of sorts."

During the Jacobite rising of 1745, Edinburgh was briefly occupied by the Jacobite "Highland Army" before its march into England. After its eventual defeat at Culloden, there followed a period of reprisals and pacification, largely directed at the rebellious clans.

In Edinburgh, the Town Council, keen to emulate Georgian London, stimulate prosperity and re-affirm its belief in the Union, initiated city improvements and expansion north and south of the castle.

Although the idea of a northwards expansion had been first mooted around 1680, during the Duke of York's residence at Holyrood, the immediate catalyst for change was a decision by the Convention of Royal Burghs in 1752 to propose improvements to the capital for the benefit of commerce.

The convention issued a pamphlet entitled Proposals for carrying on certain Public Works in the City of Edinburgh, believed to have been authored by the classical scholar Sir Gilbert Elliot and heavily influenced by the ideas of Lord Provost George Drummond.

Elliot described the existing town as follows: " Placed upon a ridge of a hill, it admits but of one good street, running from east to west, and even this is tolerably accessible only from one quarter. The narrow lanes leading to the north and south, by reason of their steepness, narrowness and dirtiness, can only be considered as so many unavoidable nuisances. Confined by the small compass of the walls, and the narrow limits of the royalty, which scarcely extends beyond the walls, the houses stand more crowded than in any other town in Europe, and are built to a height that is almost incredible."

The proposals for improvement envisaged the building of a new Exchange for merchants (now the City Chambers), new law courts and an advocates' library, expansion north and southwards, and the draining of the Nor Loch.

As the New Town to the north took shape, the Town Council expressed its loyalty to the Union and the Hanoverian monarch George III in its choice of street names e.g. Rose Street and Thistle Street; and for the royal family, George Street, Queen Street, Hanover Street, Frederick Street and Princes Street (in honour of George's two sons).

The profession of architect flourished, as did the prestige of builders, engineers and surveyors. Some of these specialists in Edinburgh successfully brought their reputations to practice in London.

From the late-1760s onwards, the professional and business classes gradually deserted the Old Town in favour of the more desirable "one-family" residences of the New Town, with separate attic or basement accommodation for domestic servants. This migration changed the social character of Edinburgh.

The Old Town became an abode of the poor. Observing conditions there in the 1770s, a widely travelled English visitor already reported that, "No people in the World undergo greater hardships, or live in a worse degree of wretchedness and poverty, than the lower classes here." From 1802 onwards a 'Second New Town' developed north of James Craig's original New Town.

Union with England in 1707 meant the end of the Scottish Parliament and saw members of parliament, aristocrats and placemen move to London. Scottish law, however, remained entirely separate from English law, with the result that the law courts and legal profession continued to exist in Edinburgh; as did the university and medical establishments.

Lawyers, Presbyterian divines, professors, medical men and architects, formed a new intellectual middle-class elite that dominated the city and facilitated the Scottish Enlightenment.

From the late 1740s onwards, Edinburgh began to gain an international reputation as a centre of ideas, especially in philosophy, history, science, economics and medicine. The Faculty of Medicine at the University of Edinburgh, formed in 1726, soon attracted students from across Britain and the American colonies.

Its chief sponsor was Archibald Campbell (1682-1761), 1st earl of Islay, later 3rd Duke of Argyll, Scotland's most influential political leader. It served as a model for

ABOVE 18th Century Image of Edinburgh Castle and the Old Town, 1769

the medical school at the University of Pennsylvania in Philadelphia.

Leading thinkers of the period included David Hume, Adam Smith, James Hutton, Joseph Black, John Playfair, William Robertson, Adam Ferguson, and jurists Lord Kames and Lord Monboddo. They often met for intense discussions at The Select Society and, later, The Poker Club.

The Royal Society of Edinburgh, founded in 1783, became Scotland's national academy of science and letters. The historian Bruce Lenman stated that their "central achievement was a new capacity to recognize and interpret social patterns."

The Edinburgh Musical Society was constituted in 1728 by well-to-do music lovers. They built St Cecilia's Hall in Niddry Street in 1763 as their private concert hall. They sponsored professional musicians and opened the concerts to their womenfolk. Flautist and composer Francesco Barsanti (1690–1772) was hired at a salary of £50. The Society had close links to the city's Masonic lodges; it was dissolved in 1797.

Influential visitors to Edinburgh included Benjamin Franklin of Philadelphia who came in 1759 and 1771 to meet with leading scientists and thinkers. Franklin, who was hosted by his close friend David Hume, concluded that the university possessed "a set of truly great men, Professors of Several Branches of Knowledge, as have ever appeared in any age or country."

The novelist Smollett had one of his characters in The Expedition of Humphrey Clinker described the city as a "hotbed of genius". Thomas Jefferson, writing to the philosopher Dugald Stewart in June 1789, declared that, as far as science was concerned, "no place in the world can pretend to a competition with Edinburgh".

From 1820 the city acquired its title of the "Modern Athens" and "Athens of the North" because of a perceived similarity in topography, the neo-classical architecture of its new public buildings and New Town, and not least its reputation as an intellectual centre.

Although Edinburgh's traditional industries of printing, brewing and distilling continued to grow in the 19th century and were joined by new firms in rubber, engineering, and pharmaceuticals, there was little industrialisation compared with other cities in Britain. By 1821, Edinburgh had been overtaken by Glasgow as Scotland's largest city.

Glasgow had benefited initially from the Atlantic trade with North America, and now became a major manufacturing centre of the British Empire. Edinburgh's city centre between Princes Street and George Street became a predominantly commercial and shopping district, sweeping away most of the original Georgian architecture of that part of the New Town. This development was partly stimulated by the advent of railways penetrating the city centre from east and west in the 1840s.

In the meantime the Old Town continued to decay into an increasingly dilapidated, overcrowded slum with high mortality rates, and was practically segregated socially from the rest of the city.

This was especially true where the subdivision of tenements offered the cheapest lodgings in narrow alleyways that formed the backdrop to the infamous 'West Port Murders' of Burke and Hare.

Following the publication of Dr. Henry Littlejohn's report on the sanitary conditions of the City of Edinburgh in 1865, major street improvements were carried out in the Old Town under Lord Provost William Chambers, and the Edinburgh City Improvement Act of 1867 initiated the transformation of the area into the predominantly Victorian Old Town seen today.

In contrast to the New Town many of the buildings were in the mock-Jacobean architectural style known as Scots Baronial, which has been described as a particularly Scottish contribution to the Gothic

TRANSACTIONS
OF THE
ROYAL SOCIETY OF EDINBURGH.
VOL. I.

EDINBURGH:
PRINTED FOR J. DICKSON, BOOKSELLER TO THE ROYAL SOCIETY.
SOLD IN LONDON BY T. CADELL, IN THE STRAND.
M.DCC.LXXXVIII.

LEFT The cover of a 1788 volume of the journal *Transaction of the Royal Society of Edinburgh*. This is the issue where James Hutton published his Theory of the Earth

Revival in keeping with the perceived "medieval" character of the Old Town.

Slum clearance brought about a fall in the death rate, but the lack of new inexpensive housing led to other poor districts becoming more overcrowded and degenerating into slums. The experience demonstrated to reformers that future projects had to include cheap new housing.

In the intellectual sphere, from 1832 to 1844, Chambers' Edinburgh Journal was the most read periodical in Britain, with a circulation over 80,000. Edited by the Chambers brothers, Robert and William, it applied the philosophy of utilitarianism to practical issues. The articles examined a wide range of social problems including poverty, alcoholism, illiteracy, sanitation, working conditions, crime, and mental illness.

During the First World War, Edinburgh was bombed on the night of 2–3 April 1916. Two German Zeppelins dropped high explosive and incendiary bombs on, among other places, Leith, the Mound, Lothian Road, the Castle Rock and the Grassmarket. Eleven civilian were killed and there were numerous injuries and extensive property damage.

Owing to its comparative lack of industry, Edinburgh was not targeted as part of the German bombing campaign against British cities in the early part of the Second World War. The port of Leith was hit on 22 July 1940 when a 1000 lb. bomb fell on the Albert Dock, though it is unclear whether the originally intended target had been the well-defended Rosyth Dockyard.

Bombs were dropped on at least 11 other occasions between June 1940 and July 1942 in what appear to have been opportunistic attacks by bombers jettisoning their remaining load while returning from the main target, possibly Clydebank or Belfast. The city therefore escaped major loss of life and damage during the war and emerged from it almost completely unscathed.

More piecemeal improvements to the Old Town followed in the early 20th century at the instigation of the pioneering town planner Patrick Geddes, who described his work as "conservative surgery", but a period of relative economic stagnation through the two world wars and their aftermaths saw its fabric deteriorate further before major slum clearance in the 1960s and 1970s began to reverse the process.

Even so, its population dropped by over two-thirds (to 3000) between 1950 and 1975; and of 292 houses in the Cowgate in 1920 only eight remained in 1980. In the mid-1960s, the working-class area of Dumbiedykes was swept away almost overnight and the George Square area, which represented the major part of the city's original southwards expansion in the 18th century, fell victim to new university building developments.

The mediaeval suburb of Potterrow, which lay outside the town walls and had been rebuilt in the Victorian period, was obliterated in the process. By the late 1960s, such developments perceived by many as unsympathetic to the historical character of the city, together with the further remodelling of sections of Princes Street, prompted the eminent historian Christopher Smout to urge its citizens "to save the New Town from the vandalism of neglect and development carried on today with the consent of the present council, whose crocodile tears and pretty exhibitions do nothing at all to stop the builders' rape of the capital".

Since the 1990s, a new financial district, including a new Edinburgh International Conference Centre, has grown up out of demolished railway property to the west of the castle; stretching in to Fountainbridge, a run-down 19th century industrial suburb

that has undergone radical change since the 1980s with the demise of industrial and brewery premises.

This burgeoning development has enabled Edinburgh to stay at the forefront of financial and administrative services – second only to London – and indeed now account for a third of all commercial office space in the city.

The development of Edinburgh Park, a new 38-acre business and technology park to the west of the city centre, has also greatly contributed to the city's major economic regeneration.

ABOVE Western end of Grassmarket with Edinburgh Castle behind, painted in 1845

Chapter 5

Historic Places of Interest

PORTCULLIS GATE

James Douglas, fourth Earl of Morton and regent of Scotland ordered the construction of the Portcullis Gate after the Lang Siege. It is built on the ruined 14th century Constable's Tower and acted as a formidable obstacle to any would-be attackers.

THE GREAT HALL

The Great Hall was completed in 1511 for James IV. It served as the main hall for the assemblies in the castle; during the occupation of Cromwell in the 1650s the hall was converted into soldiers' barracks and enlarged in 1737 so as to accommodate 312 men. After the building of the new barracks in 1796, the Great Hall was

converted into a hospital until 1887.

The architect Hippolyte Blanc restored the Great Hall and is largely responsible for much of the way that it looks today.

QUEEN ANN BUILDING

During the later Middle Ages, this location had been used to serve as kitchens to the Great Hall as well as to the Gunhouse. The design of the present building is thought to have been inspired by the French invasion scare of 1708 and was to provide the quarters for staff officers; it also accommodated the barrack master, master gunner, schoolmaster and chaplain. In 1933, it was rebuilt and became the naval and military Museum to complement the Scottish National War Memorial.

SCOTTISH NATIONAL WAR MEMORIAL

In 14th July 1927, the Prince of Wales opened this building as a memorial to the Scottish dead of the First World War.

On the site of the memorial used to stand St Mary's Church from the Middle Ages. However, in 1540 it was converted into a munitions house; this was then demolished in 1755 to make room for the North Barracks.

ABOVE LEFT
The Great Hall,
Edinburgh Castle

ABOVE RIGHT The
Queen Anne Building
(centre-right),
Edinburgh Castle

THE ROYAL PALACE

This Palace was the official residence of the later Stuart kings and queens of Scotland. James VI and I of England were born at the Royal Palace in June 1566 in a small chamber room known as Queen Mary's room.

During the Lang Siege, the Palace was

By 1863, Robert Billings was appointed to give the building a more picturesque appearance. When the army vacated the building in 1923, Sir Robert Lorimer adapted it as the national shrine. The building is also used to commemorate the men who fell in the Second World War.

severely battered, however in 1617 it was remodelled both inside and out for the homecoming of James VI. The Royal Palace is now home to the Honours of Scotland, the Scottish Crown Jewels that are displayed in the Crown Room along with the Stone of Destiny. This is Scotland's Coronation Stone which was returned to Scotland in 1996.

ST MARGARET'S CHAPEL

This chapel was built by King David I in 1110 and is probably the oldest structure still standing in the castle today. It was built to commemorate King David's mother who had died in the Castle in 1093. Until the 16th century, the Royals had used it as a private place of prayer; however it then became a gunpowder store.

It was restored as a chapel in 1845. The chapel houses beautiful stained glass windows which were designed by Douglas Strachan: they depict St Andrew, St Columba, St Margaret and Sir William Wallace and were installed in 1922.

THE ONE O'CLOCK GUN

Every day, the One O'Clock Gun is fired at precisely one o'clock. The original

ABOVE
St Margaret's Chapel,
Edinburgh Castle

LEFT
The One O'clock Gun

ABOVE
Mons Meg is a
medieval bombard
located at Edinburgh
Castle

tradition came from the sailing ships being able to check and reset their chronometers in the days before accurate timepieces were available.

The time ball, still seen today on top of Nelson's Monument at Carlton Hill, was invented by a Scottish naval officer in 1861. At precisely one o'clock the ball drops giving the signal to sailors.

MONS MEG

Mons Meg was presented to King James II by his uncle the Duke of Burgundy in 1457. It is one of the two surviving bombard guns and the name Mons comes from where they were made in present-day Belgium.

The canon weighs six tons and is

capable of firing cannon balls weighing 150 kg nearly two miles. Although it was used in action against the English at Norham Castle on the River Tweed, it was impractical to drag around because of its great weight so was therefore retired to Edinburgh Castle where it was used to fire the salute celebrating the marriage of Mary Queen of Scots to the French Dauphin, Francis.

The last time Mons Meg was fired was on 14th October 1681, celebrating the birthday of the Duke of Albany and York, who was later to become King James VII of Scotland and II of England. The gun now is situated outside St Margaret's Chapel where it has been since 1829.

CROWN SQUARE

The Crown Square within the walls of Edinburgh Castle served as the main courtyard. Dating back from the 15th century, it was built on the south facing slopes of Castle Rock, where underneath the artificial platform are a series of great stone vaults. Originally called Palace Yard, the square was renamed after the discovery of the Scottish Crown Jewels in 1818.

WITCHES WELL

The Witches Well is situated at the entrance to the castle on the West Wall, a cast iron water fountain commemorates the death of more than 300 women who were burned at the stake, accused of being witches. During the 16th century,

ABOVE
Sir Walter Scott
and the Governor
of Edinburgh Castle
rediscover Scotland's
'lost' Crown, Sceptre
and Sword of State
in 1818. A tableau in
the Castle

more witch burnings were carried out at the castle than anywhere else in the country. Cruelly, the victims were often tortured brutally before being put to death at the stake.

THE HONOURS OF SCOTLAND

Within the Crown Room, sits the ancient Honours of Scotland, the Crown, the Sceptre and Sword of State. King James I in 1540 remodeled the Crown; the Crown was made from Scottish gold mined from the Crawford Moor mine. It is intricately decorated and thought to have been made by French craftsmen.

The Sceptre was a gift from the Pope to King James IV in 1494; this was again remodelled by King James V who added his initials to the Sceptre. A cut and polished rock crystal forms the globe of the Sceptre with a Scottish pearl on the top.

The Sword of State was again another gift from the Pope of the day to James IV in 1507. The blade of the sword is one metre long and includes a sword belt and consecrated hat.

THE STONE OF DESTINY

The Stone of Destiny is also known as the Stone of Scone and although looking like an ordinary piece of sandstone, it has deep symbolic meaning and centuries of Anglo Scottish rivalry.

The stone had been used as the traditional Coronation Seat for Scottish kings and queens for centuries. The last Scottish monarch to be crowned on the stone was King Edward Balliol in 1292 however it was then stolen by King Edward I, known as the Hammer of the Scots and taken to Westminster Abbey.

A group of Scottish Nationalists stole the stone back in 1950, but it was soon returned. In 1996, on St Andrew's Day, The Stone of Destiny was returned from Westminster Abbey and is now to be seen in the Crown Room at Edinburgh Castle.

CASTLE ESPLANADE

In 1753, the large flat area in front of the Gate House was built as a parade ground for resident troops. In modern times, it has come to be used as the outdoor stage for the Military Tattoo and

has occasionally hosted large pop and rock concerts with the castle being lit up behind to form an impressive backdrop.

HOLYROOD PALACE

Holyrood Palace was planned to be the official residence of the British monarchs in Scotland. It is at the end of the Royal Mile in Edinburgh, opposite Edinburgh Castle and has been the principal residence for many kings and queens of Scotland since the 16th century; it is also used for state occasions and official entertaining.

It was King David I in 1128, who founded Holyrood Abbey. The proximity of the abbey to Edinburgh Castle meant that it was continually visited by Scotland's monarchs who lodged in the guesthouse which was situated in one of the abbey cloisters.

In the early 16th century, King James IV built a new palace adjoining the

Abbey and King James V also made additions to this which included the present north-west tower. It was the architect Sir William Bruce who reconstructed Holyrood Palace between 1671 and 1679 in Baroque design.

Within the shell of the former Holyrood Free Church and Duchess of Gordon's School now stands the Queen's Gallery, which was built in the 1840s, opening to the public in 2002 to exhibit works of art from the Royal Collection.

At the beginning of each summer, Queen Elizabeth resides at Holyrood Palace for one week and carries out a range of official engagements and ceremonies.

The original 16th century historic apartments belonging to Mary Queen of Scots and the State apartments are mainly open to the public throughout the year; however, they are closed when being used for official and state entertaining and when the members of the Royal family are in residence.

Within the grounds of the palace is the ruined Augustinian abbey which had been founded in 1128 by King David I. This became an important administrative centre, with a Papal legate being received here in 1177.

In 1326, Robert the Bruce held a parliament at the abbey and it is thought that by 1329 the abbey may have already been in use as a royal residence.

BELOW Palace of Holyroodhouse

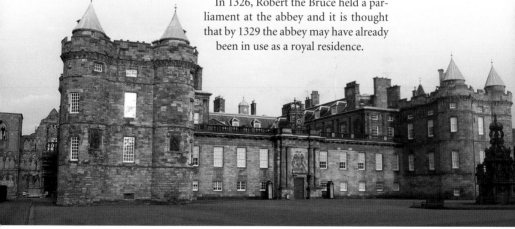

HISTORIC PLACES OF INTEREST

King David II became the first king of Scots to be buried at Holyrood in 1370. King James II was born in Holyrood in 1430; he was also crowned, married and laid to rest in the Abbey.

King James IV built the Gothic palace which stood adjacent to the Abbey between 1501 and 1505. The palace itself contained a chapel, gallery, royal apartments and a great hall; it was built around the quadrangle just west of the abbey cloister.

When the palace was reconstructed by King James V, a new chapel was built and the old one converted into the council chamber for ceremonial visits.

Holyrood was looted and burned by the Earl of Hertford in the 1500s. Repairs were made, however, the altars had been destroyed by a Reforming mob in 1559. After the Scottish Reformation, many of the abbey buildings became neglected with the choir and transepts of the abbey church being pulled down in 1570.

When Mary Queen of Scots returned to Scotland in 1561, she erected archery butts in her private garden to practice her archery and hunted deer in Holyrood Park.

Oliver Cromwell's soldiers were thought to have set parts of the palace on fire in 1650s and afterwards they were effectively abandoned, the remains being used as barracks.

When King Charles II was restored as King of England and Scotland, repairs were put aside by the Privy Council to rebuild Holyrood.

Many grace and favour apartments were built in the Palace and in 1670 Lord Hatton became the first of Noble to take up an apartment. The original architect, Sir William Bruce was cancelled in 1678 and Lord Hatton oversaw the remaining work.

Sadly, the palace began to lose its principal functions after the Union of Scotland and England in 1707. Although many nobles still continued to use their grace and favour apartments, the king's apartments were neglected.

In October 1745, Bonnie Prince Charlie held court at Holyrood for five weeks during the Jacobite rising; he occupied the Duke of Hamilton's apartments rather than the neglected king's apartments and held his court in the Gallery.

Many royal portraits in the gallery were damaged when government troops were billeted in the Palace after the Battle of Falkirk. In 1768, the roof of the abbey church collapsed and can be seen in this state today.

By the 16th century, the precincts of Holyrood Abbey were designated as a debtor's sanctuary, The residents were known as the Abbie Lairds, only being able to leave the sanctuary on Sundays as no arrests were permitted on the Sabbath.

After the French Revolution, the Comte d'Artois (later to be King Charles X of France) came to live at Holyrood, taking advantage of the abbey sanctuary to avoid his debtors. During this time, the king's apartments were renovated.

King George IV visited Holyrood in 1822 and ordered repairs to the palace; however, he stipulated that Queen Mary's rooms should be protected from any changes.

In 1834 King William IV made the agreement that the High Commissioner to the general assembly of the Church of Scotland could use the palace during the sitting of the assembly, a tradition that continues to this day.

During Queen Victoria's first visit to Scotland in 1842 she was prevented from visiting Holyrood because of an outbreak of scarlet fever. However by 1850, the Queen took up residence; her husband Prince Albert took a keen interest in the grounds and ordered a new carriage drive to the north and garden which exists to this day.

BELOW Holyrood from Calton Hil, 1878

ABOVE The dining room in Holyrood Palace

According to local myth, the palace is said to be haunted by the naked ghost of Agnes Sampson who had been accused of witchcraft and stripped and tortured in 1592. She is locally known as "bald Agnes."

Today, the palace is mainly the work of the late 17th century, with the exception being the North West tower which is 16th century.

In the 17th century apartments, there are beautiful Italian paintings by Lattanzii Gambara painted around 1550. These had been bought by Prince Albert in 1856.

In the Great Gallery can be found 110 portraits of Scottish monarchs dating from 330 BC. It was Bonnie Prince Charlie who held many evening balls in the gallery; however, later it became a Catholic chapel, and the gallery is now used for large public functions including investitures and banquets.

Within the North West Tower is the oratory of Queen Mary; this was the scene of the murder of David Rizzio who had been dragged from the supper table in the Northern Territory.

While the Queen is in residence, holding court in the Palace for one week every year, the Scottish variant of the Royal Standard of the United Kingdom is flown from the turrets of the palace.

It was George V who transformed Holyrood into a 20th century palace, he had central heating and electric lighting installed before his visit in 1911 and also formally designated it as the monarchs official residence in Scotland, it then became the location for regular royal ceremonies and events. Holyrood House is still the property of the Crown and is maintained by the Property section of the Royal Household.

THE SCOTTISH PARLIAMENT BUILDING

The Scottish Parliament Building can be found to the east of the city centre, on the edge of the Old Town. Its boundary is marked by the Canongate stretch of the Royal Mile and is close to the Palace of Holyrood House, bordered by Holyrood Park. To the south, can be found the slopes of Salisbury Crags and Arthur's Seat. It was previously the headquarters of the Scottish & Newcastle Brewery.

The construction of the Scottish parliament building began in 1999, with the first debate in the new building being held by the members of the Scottish parliament (MSPs) in September 2004, the queen presided at the formal opening which took place on 9th October 2004.

Before the new building was completed, the Scottish parliament had been held in the general assembly hall which is on the Mound in Edinburgh. All office and administrative support

BELOW Scottish Parliament and Calton Hill, from Salisbury Crags. The roof line of the Parliament intended to evoke the crags of the Scottish landscape and, in places, upturned fishing boats. Solar panels can also be seen, part of the building's sustainability strategy

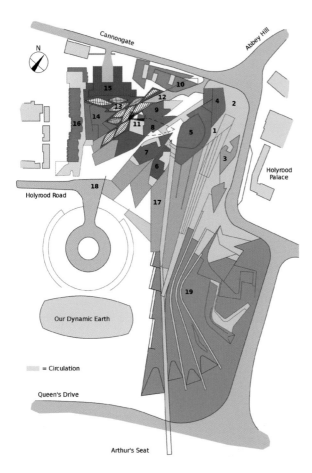

for the Parliament had been provided in buildings leased from the city of Edinburgh Council; the new Scottish Parliament Building brought together all the elements of the parliament into one purpose-built complex which can house 129 MSPs and more than 1000 staff and civil servants.

The building and construction of the Scottish Parliament Building have been dogged by controversy. There have been many criticisms by both petitions, media and the general Scottish public alike over the choices, architect design and construction companies that were chosen.

The building was finished over three years late and at a cost of £414 million, the original estimate being between £10 and £40 million. During a major public enquiry into the whole affair, it was concluded that the management of the project was wholly inept.

Although the aim of the Scottish Parliamentary Building was to create a union between both the Scottish landscape, its people, its culture and the city of Edinburgh, the public reaction to it has been mixed, with the building being fourth in a UK poll asking which buildings the public would most like to see demolished.

The building itself was designed to

house a number of sustainability features and was located on a Brownfield site close to many areas of public transport. The building houses renewable sources and solar panels from the Canongate building are used for heating the water.

There is a high level of insulation which helps to keep the building warm during winter months, however this has caused problems during the summer with the building remaining too warm and standard solutions to cool the building use high energy programs.

However, natural ventilation is used wherever possible and a computerised management system is used to automatically open windows to cool the building during the summer.

The debating chamber within the Scottish Parliament Building is made in the shape of a horseshoe, with the governing party sitting in the middle of the semicircle, opposition parties sitting on either side. The intention of this is to blur the political divisions and encourage consensus.

As the members of Scottish parliament enter the chamber, they all pass under a stone lintel which was once part of the pre 1707 Parliament building called the Arniston Stone, this is a nice symbolic connection between the historical Parliament of Scotland and the present day modern Scottish Parliament.

At the centre of the complex is the Garden Lobby which connects the debating chambers, committee rooms and administrative

OPPOSITE Site plan of the Scottish Parliament:

1 - Public Entrance
2 - Plaza
3 - Pond
4 - Press Tower
5 - Debating Chamber
6 - Tower one
7 - Tower two
8 - Tower three
9 - Tower four
10 - Tower five, Cannongate Bldg.
11 - Main Staircase
12 - MSP's Entrance
13 - Lobby
14 - Garden
15 - Queensbery House
16 - MSP building
17 - Turf roof
18 - Carpark and vehiclular entrance
19 - Landscaped park

LEFT View of the roofing structure of the debating chamber, where seating is arranged in a hemicycle rather than the adversarial layout of other Westminster style legislatures

offices with Queensberry House and the MSP building.

The Garden Lobby has been constructed with roof lights made from stainless steel with all the glass work covered by solid oak lattice struts, this allows for much natural light in the building and it is used for television interviews, social gatherings and official events. It has been described as «one of the great processional routes in contemporary architecture.

Other buildings include the MSP building which contains the offices for each MSP; it is over four and six stories in height and granite clad. It has unusual windows which have been inspired by the repeated leaf motif and the Scottish traditional stepped gable, each office has a bay window with seats and shelving in order to provide the MSPs a place for contemplation in privacy and in shade from the sun. However some MSPs have complained that the offices are too dark with the majority of natural light being removed.

Along with criticism aimed at the cost and lateness of the Scottish Parliament Building, the choice of site and use of a non-Scottish architect has made the project very controversial.

SCOTT MONUMENT

Standing in the Princes Street Gardens is a Victorian Gothic monument celebrating the life of Sir Walter Scott, Edinburgh's famous author who wrote such books as Ivanhoe, Rob Roy and the Lady of the Lake.

The tower was commissioned in 1841 with construction taking nearly four years. It is over 61 metres high and has many narrow spiral staircases which give beautiful panoramic views of central Edinburgh and its surrounds.

In the 1990s it was decided that the stonework on the tower should be cleaned, however after much debate the decision was taken not to clean the stone due to concerns to how much damage this would cause. Instead, a restoration programme has been initiated, it has replaced old repairs and damaged areas with the original Binny stone, the original quarry had to be reopened to provide enough material for the project. Both the Heritage Lottery Fund, Historic Scotland and the City of Edinburgh Council funded the cost for the restoration which exceeded £2 million.

ARTHUR'S SEAT

Within the 640-acre Royal Park, adjacent to Holyrood Palace lies a dormant volcano sitting 251m above sea level. The highest point is called Arthur›s Seat; it is the site of a large and well preserved fort and gives excellent views of the city.

LEFT The Sir Walter Scott statue designed by John Steell, located inside the Scott Monument

The name is supposed to have been derived from the legendary king Arthur, however it's true origin is unknown.

Five boys hunting for rabbits in a cave on the crags of Arthur's Seat made a rather gory discovery in 1836. They found a set of 17 miniature coffins which contained small wooden figures. No one is sure why they had been placed there, however it is believed they may have been made for witchcraft or possibly be connected with the murders committed by Burke and Hare in 1828. The little coffins can now be viewed in Edinburgh's Royal Museum.

NATIONAL MONUMENT

Upon the summit of Calton Hill, with views down to Princes Street and the city below, is the National Monument which was built to commemorate the Scottish soldiers and sailors who died fighting in the Napoleonic wars (1803-1815).

In 1822, a six ton foundation stone was laid by King George IV and the celebrated architect William Playfair was employed to build a monument in the appearance of the Parthenon on the Athenian Acropolis, Edinburgh at the time being affectionately known as the Athens of the North. The plans were deemed extraordinarily ambitious, with the building to have the external quality of the Parthenon but to operate as a church with catacombs underneath.

Many prominent figures such as Sir Walter Scott, Lord Elgin and Lord Cockburn helped to promote the project, however with only one third of the total funds needed, the decision to commence work was taken in 1826.

Each of the monuments 12 colossal Doric columns were hugely difficult to install, requiring the brute force of 12 horses and 70 men to carry the stone from Craigleith Quarry to the summit of Calton Hill, which is more than 3 miles in distance. Over 300 men were working on the monument when in 1829, funding for the project dried up and

BELOW Tourists posing at the National Monument of Scotland

RIGHT Statue of
Greyfriars Bobby

the work was abandoned.

In later years, several attempts to revive the building were carried out but it is still very much unfinished and is now widely known as 'Edinburgh's Disgrace.' When the city of Glasgow offered to help complete the project, Edinburgh declined, which initiated the other nickname for the monument - the pride and the proverty.

GREYFRIARS BOBBY

In 1850, a gardener named John Gray arrived in Edinburgh with his family, to avoid the workhouse he became a night watchman for the Edinburgh police force. Keeping him company through long winter nights as his little Skye terrier called Bobby. They became a familiar sight walking the old cobbled streets of Edinburgh.

When John eventually died of tuberculosis in 1858, he was buried at Greyfriars Kirkyard. His little dog refused to leave his Master's grave even in the worst weather conditions.

After many attempts to evict Bobby, in the end of the gardener and keeper of Greyfriars placed some sacking beneath two table stands at the side of John's grave and the little dog became famous, keeping constant watch and guard over his Master's grave for 14 years.

When Baroness Angelia Georgina Burdett Coutts, President of the Ladies Committee of the RSPCA heard of the story, she requested from the City Council their permission to erect a granite fountain of the statue of Bobby.

This was granted and sculptor William Brady was commissioned to create the statue which features the headstone that reads: "Greyfriars Bobby, died 14th January 1872 aged 18 years, let his loyalty and devotion be a lesson to us all."

THE ROYAL MILE

The Royal Mile starts from the entrance of Edinburgh Castle and leads down to the gates of Holyrood Palace. It is actually 107 yards more than a mile, and several streets connect up to it to make up the Royal Mile. These include Castle Hill, Lawnmarket, High Street, Canongate and Abbey Strand which leads to Holyrood Palace.

There have been people living on the Royal Mile at Castle Hill for the last 7000 years.

In 1124, King David I visited the hill fort on the crag which was then supplying goods to local nobleman, soldiers and monks in the fort. At this time it was known as the Burgh of Eiden.

The King granted trading rights to the township and also the Lawnmarket which went on to become the open air trading market. It is thought that he set out the high street which was referred to as Via Regis meaning the Way of the King, possibly being where the name Royal Mile originates. The Royal Mile thrived, grand timber buildings being constructed and named after the landowners in the area; most enclosures had large gardens which would have housed livestock of the day. Sadly, in 1544 King Henry VIII of England who had ordered its destruction when trying to force the Scots to allow his son to marry the infant Mary Queen of Scots destroyed this mediaeval Garden city.

The houses were built in stone but by 1591 the overcrowded conditions made to the area increasingly unsanitary, only within the Canongate were there still to be found the large mansions with lovely gardens for use by the nobility.

The overcrowding became worse by 1645 with over 70,000 people living within the Royal Mile. Many buildings were 14 stories high with over 300 people living in one block, sometimes with ten people sharing a single room. Street cleaning wasn't enforced until the end of the 18th century.

It was the Lord Provost William Chambers who, in 1865, began to initiate the improvement to the living conditions in the Royal Mile by extensive modern restorations and the building of new tenements on Blackfriars Street and on St Mary's Street.

In the 1880s, town planner and botanist Patrick Geddes also helped to improve the area by remodelling the Canongate section and the top of the mound. He went on to design courtyards and gardens more in keeping with the original Royal Mile.

HISTORIC PLACES OF INTEREST

Chapter 6

Ghastly Goings On

In 1828 a series of murders were committed in Edinburgh famously becoming called the West Port murders. The murderers were two Irish immigrants called William Burke and William Hare one of the deadliest double acts in the history of heartless crimes.

Both men had emigrated to Scotland and worked as navvies on the Union Canal. Whilst they were working at the Edinburgh terminus of the canal, Hare married Margaret Laird who ran a lodging house. The two met and quickly became good friends.

At that time, Edinburgh was renowned for being the spearhead of medical science; however, the cadavers that were required for research purposes were few on the ground in the early 1800s and only five corpses were allocated to the Edinburgh Medical College for medical research purposes each year. A famous Edinburgh College doctor, Robert Knox, started to pay for illegally consumed corpses, and very soon after this, bodysnatching became big business.

Ordinary Edinburgh residents were so revolted by this that it was common for recently buried relatives to be watched over 24 hours a day until the corpse was deemed too decomposed for the body snatchers to sell.

In many of Edinburgh's graveyards, high walls and watchtowers to keep out the body snatchers became commonplace and examples can still be seen to this day in St Cuthberts at the top of King Stables Road.

When an old resident from Mary's lodging house died, Burke and Hare decided to sell the body to Dr. Robert Knox. They both seized upon the opportunity to make money out of finding and selling bodies but no longer waited for their victims to die of natural causes.

Their first victims were tenants from the boarding houses but they quickly moved on to prostitutes and strangers they met on the streets of Edinburgh. Burke and Hare's method of murder was that of suffocation that later became known as "Burking."

Eventually their crimes were detected when a body was found under the bed of

ABOVE LEFT
Skeleton of William Burke

ABOVE RIGHT
Execution of William Burke

OPPOSITE Hare's Lodging House

Burke. Even though they offered a £10 a week bribe, the witness reported the crime to the authorities.

Hare was offered immunity in return for testifying against his accomplice Burke; he was found guilty and was hanged in Edinburgh on January 1829. The Edinburgh medical College then publicly dissected his body; his skeleton still remains on display at the college museum and rather more gruesomely a book was made from his skin which is still in the Police Museum on the Royal Mile in Edinburgh.

Hare fled to England and was last seen some years later in Carlisle. Dr. Robert Knox was never prosecuted as no proof could be given that he knew the corpses he bought were murder victims.

GHASTLY GOINGS ON

RIGHT Mary King's Close, Edinburgh

The gruesome Burke and Hare murders were to become a catalyst for changes in the way that cadavers were procured for medical science. In 1830, the Anatomy Act allowed for the supply to be increased to combat the trade in corpses across Britain as a whole.

MARY KING'S CLOSE

This 17th century close was named after Mary Queen of Scots. It is one of the many underground streets that had been built over during the modernisation of Edinburgh with the lower floor acting as the foundation for the world exchange, built in 1753.

Tragedy struck in 1645 when the plague was prevalent in Edinburgh. It is said that the local council made a terrible decision to contain the plague by bricking up the close for several years and leaving the inhabitants to die inside, earning it the nickname of "Street of Sorrows."

There are some myths surrounding the ghost of a little girl named Annie who had lost her favourite doll. She has now become something of a local celebrity and visitors have left a room full of toys for her.

DUKE OF QUEENSBURY

Queensbury house, which was built in 1667 and bought by the first Duke of Queensbury in 1689, is now a listed building in the Canongate on the Royal mile but has rather a ghoulish history.

The second Duke of Queensbury's son, James, who was said to be insane, was left chained in the ground floor rooms but one day escaped. His father returned home to find his lunatic son was devouring the flesh of the young kitchen boy who was still roasting on the spit. The ghost of the kitchen boy is said to haunt the building.

NOR'LOCH

To strengthen Edinburgh Castle's northern defences, King James III ordered the ground between the Old Town and Princes Street to be flooded. In the east, a dam was built and the natural spring water from the St Margaret's well was used to flood the valley.

This became a relaxing haven for the residents of Edinburgh who used the lake for boating in the summer and skating in the winter.

Unfortunately, the lake then became a convenient dump for all sorts of waste including human excrement and quickly became a stinking cesspool. The health of the local residents became affected, with methane gas causing many to have hallucinations.

In the 18th century, Scotland became

obsessed with witchcraft and many suspected witches were "douked" in the lock. This consisted of the poor woman having her hands and toes tied together and ducked on a specially designed stool twice into the loch.

If she drowned, she would be found innocent, however if she lived long enough to float and survive the drowning, she would be burned at the stake on Castle Hill.

In 1759 the problem became so bad that a decision was made to drain the loch. It is now the Princes Street Gardens.

TOP LEFT Arms of the 1st, 2nd and 3rd Dukes of Queensberry

ABOVE Edinburgh Castle with the Nor Loch in the foreground, c.1690. Part of an engraving by John Slezer

Universities
and Schools

THE UNIVERSITY OF EDINBURGH

The University of Edinburgh was founded in 1583 is the sixth oldest in the world yet it is still regarded as one of the most famous and prestigious.

During Edinburgh's Age of Enlightenment, the university helped to give the city the nickname of the *Athens of the North*, with famous attendees including the naturalist Charles Darwin; inventor Alexander Graham Bell; first president of Tanzania Julius Nyerere; as well as famous authors such as Sir Arthur Conan Doyle, Robert Louis Stevenson, J.M. Barrie and Sir Walter Scott.

The university has also produced 18 Nobel Prize winners, three UK Prime Ministers, two current UK Supreme Court Justices and several Olympic gold medallists.

The British Royal Family has also had many associations with the university, Prince Philip being Chancellor from 1953 to 2010, and Princess Anne since 2011.

Over 47,000 applications are made to the university every year, although only around a quarter of all applicants are offered a place, the competition to be part of the university being very fierce.

The University was originally called the College of Law and was founded after Bishop Robert Reid of St Magnus Cathedral in Orkney left money in a legacy to start it up.

The Town Council and Ministers of the City helped to establish the college as a university by a Royal Charter which was granted by James VI in 1582.

The university's first custom-built building was the Old College, now the School of Law, which can be found on South Bridge. It was first used to teach anatomy and the developing science of surgery and was then expanded into many other subjects.

At the end of the 19th century, Old College became very overcrowded and in 1875, Robert Anderson was commissioned to design a new Medical School.

The medical school was more or less built to his design and was completed by the addition of the McEwan Hall in the 1880s.

Edinburgh University's New College was originally built as a Free Church college in the 1840s and has been the home of Divinity at the university since the 1920s.

The oldest purpose built concert hall in Scotland is the St Cecilia's Concert Hall which is owned and looked after by the university.

It also owns the oldest purpose built student union building in the world called Teviot Row House as well as the restored 17th-century Mylne›s Court student residence which is located at the head of Edinburgh›s Royal Mile.

The university library pre-dates the University by three years. It was founded in 1580 after the donation of a large book collection by Clement Littill. Indeed, the collection has grown to become the largest university library in Scotland with over two million periodicals, manuscripts, theses, microforms and printed works.

These are housed in the main university library building in George Square – one of the largest academic library buildings in Europe - which also includes an extensive series of Faculty and Departmental Libraries.

The two oldest Schools – Law and Divinity – are both highly esteemed in their respective subjects, with Law being based in Old College, and Divinity being based in New College, on the Mound.

Edinburgh University's medical school is renowned throughout the world and was widely regarded as the best medical school in the English-speaking world throughout the 18th century and first half of the 19th century. Indeed, the College of Medicine and Veterinary Medicine is one of the best medical institutions in the world and is considered to be the best in the UK for medical research.

Amongst its remarkable graduates are the inventor of the hypodermic syringe; the curer of scurvy; the discoverer of carbon dioxide and the isolation of nitrogen; the publisher of the theory of evolution; the inventor of the decompression chamber; and one of the pioneers of in-vitro fertilisation (IVF).

The faculty of the medical school has introduced antiseptic to sterilize surgical instruments, discovered chloroform anesthesia, discovered oxytocin, developed the Hepatitis B vaccine, co-founded Biogen, pioneered treatment for tuberculosis, and discovered apoptosis and tyramine.

The medical school has been associated with six Nobel Prize winners: five winners of the Nobel Prize in Physiology or Medicine and one winner of the Nobel Prize in Chemistry.

The University has educated many famous scientists, with one of its most notable sons being Professor of Chemistry, Joseph Black who discovered carbon dioxide and founded the world›s first Chemical Society.

The Edinburgh University Theatre Company (EUTC) started life in 1896 as the Edinburgh University Drama Society. The company runs the Bedlam Theatre which is the oldest student-run theatre in Britain as well as an award winning Edinburgh Fringe venue.

The EUTC also funds and runs an acclaimed student improvised comedy troupe called The Improverts during term time and the Fringe. Famous graduates include Ian Charleson, Michael Boyd, Kevin McKidd, and Greg Wise.

The list of famous graduates is too long to mention but some of the illustrious past pupils include Prime Ministers Gordon Brown, Lord Palmerston and Lord John Russell; astronaut Piers Sellers; engineers Alexander Graham Bell and William Rankine; naturalist Charles Darwin; writers Sir Arthur Conan Doyle, Robert Louis Stevenson, J.M. Barrie, Sir Walter Scott and Alistair Moffat; actor Ian Charleson; and former director general of MI5 Stella Rimington.

UNIVERSITY OF EDINBURGH BUSINESS SCHOOL

The University of Edinburgh Business School (UEBS) - formerly known as the University of Edinburgh Management School - is the business school of the University of Edinburgh.

In 1916, the university was encouraged by the Edinburgh Chamber of Commerce to consider instituting a degree suitable for study by its members. In 1918, the Bachelor of Commerce (BCom) was launched and a year later, the *Chair of Accounting and Business Method* was founded, the first such chair in Scotland.

Originally part of the Faculty of Arts,

these initiatives led to the creation of the *Department of Business Studies* and the *Department of Accounting and Business Method*. The BCom degree survived until the start of the 21st century before giving way to the Master of Arts (MA) in Business Studies.

The Master of Business Administration (MBA) was first offered in 1980, followed by the Part-time MBA in 1984. Since then, over 3,500 students from a wide variety of backgrounds, nationalities and business specialisms have completed these programmes. The first Master of Science (MSc) was launched in 1996.

In August 2010 the School relocated to a nearby building located at the heart of the University campus. This state-of-the-art building now houses all school staff and features eight lecture theatres, multiple syndicate rooms, an executive education suite and a cafe.

Famous Graduates from the university include Susan Deacon, (MBA) Former Health Minister in the Scottish Executive, now Professor of Social Change at Queen Margaret University; Christopher Lovelock, (BA and MA Econ) previously adjunct professor of marketing at Yale School of Management – Authority on Service management; Chris Montgomery, (MBA) ex-CEO of mp3.com Europe; Sir Brian Stewart, ex chairman of Scottish & Newcastle and of Standard Life; and Sir David Tweedie, (BCom and PhD) ex-Chairman of the International Accounting Standards Board (IASB).

EDINBURGH NAPIER UNIVERSITY

Edinburgh Napier University was named after John Napier, the inventor of logarithms and the decimal point. He was born in 1550 in the medieval tower house of Merchiston Castle (the site of the Merchiston campus) and his statue stands in the tower of Merchiston Castle.

In 1966, the university was renamed Napier College of Science and Technology but then three years later, it merged with the Sighthill-based Edinburgh College of Commerce and formed the Napier College of Commerce and Technology, which became a Central Institution in 1985. In February 2009 the University launched its new title, Edinburgh Napier University, to reflect its location in Scotland's capital city.

The university is based around its Merchiston, Craighouse, Craiglockhart and Sighthill campuses. There are also

smaller medical campuses outside the city in Melrose and Livingston's St John's Hospital at Howden.

Edinburgh Napier includes degrees in such subjects as engineering, computing, nursing and midwifery, science, business courses, timber engineering and transport studies. It offers a range of creative courses, including film, graphic design, acting, publishing and product design.

Famous graduates of Edinburgh Napier University include Shehzad Afzal, film director and screenwriter; John Andrew Barrett, Scottish Liberal Democrat MP; Jayne Baxter, Labour party politician; James Boyle, broadcaster; and Carol Kirkwood, BBC weather forecaster; Gordon Smart, Journalist and show business editor at The Sun; and Kyle Traynor, Scottish rugby union player.

HERIOT-WATT UNIVERSITY

Heriot-Watt was established as the School of Arts of Edinburgh by Scottish businessman Leonard Horner on 16 October 1821. Inspired by Anderson's College in Glasgow, Horner wanted the School to provide practical knowledge of science and technology to Edinburgh's working men.

Originally, the institution was fairly small; giving lectures two nights a week in rented rooms and only having a small library of around 500 technical works. However, it was oversubscribed, with admissions soon closing despite the cost of 15 shillings for a year's access to lectures and the library.

The School was managed by a board of 18 directors and primarily funded by sponsors from the middle and upper classes including such famous sons of Edinburgh as Robert Stevenson and Walter Scott. It first became associated with the inventor and engineer James Watt in 1824, when the school was trying to raise funds to secure permanent accommodation.

In 1837, the School of Arts moved location to Adam Square which it then purchased in 1851 thanks to the funds raised in James Watt's name. To

UNIVERSITIES AND SCHOOLS

honour the purchase, the School changed its name to the Watt Institution and School of Arts in 1852.

In 1869 women were permitted to attend lectures at the Watt Institution for the first time. This move put the Watt Institution some way ahead of Scottish universities, who were only permitted to allow women to graduate 20 years later following the Universities (Scotland) Act of 1889. The decision to admit women was made in large part owing to pressure from local campaigner Mary Burton, who was to become the institution›s first female director in 1874.

The Watt Club was founded at the Watt Institution on 12 May 1854, and is today the oldest alumni organisation in the UK. After the unveiling of a statue of James Watt outside the Institution, local jeweller J.E Vernon proposed that: "(a club should be formed) … whose object would be to sup together on the anniversary of the birth of James Watt… and also to promote the interests of the school, by raising a fund each year to provide prizes."

The former site of Heriot-Watt College on Chambers Street is now occupied by the Edinburgh Crown Office.

Once Heriot-Watt became estab-

lished as a technical college, the new management committee made plans to extend the institution›s buildings and to strengthen its academic reputation.

The College was one of only three non-university institutions in the UK with the power to appoint professors, the first being appointed in 1887. In 1902 the College became a central institution. Two years later, the College introduced awards for graduating students which were similar to university degrees.

During World War I, the student numbers dropped as most young men enlisted, while teaching in engineering was delayed as the department was used for the manufacture of shells and munitions. During World War II, again student numbers dropped with the electrical engineering department became involved in training the armed services in the use of radar.

In 1951, the College introduced a postgraduate award offering awards equivalent to university degrees and doctorates in all practical respects. In 1963 the Robbins Report recognised this, recommending that it should be awarded a university status. This recommendation was enacted in 1961 and the institution officially became Heriot-Watt University.

Heriot-Watt continued its expansion in the centre of Edinburgh after attaining university status, growing big enough to need relocation. In 1966 Midlothian Council gifted the Riccarton estate in South West Edinburgh to the University and in 1969 work began to build the site of the future campus. The process of relocation to Riccarton continued until 1992, teaching and facilities were divided between the new campus and the city centre until the new campus was completed.

The University has continued to grow after its move to Riccarton, with the construction of additional student halls, a sports centre and a postgraduate centre. The institution has now also expanded beyond Edinburgh and merged with the Scottish College of Textiles creating a campus in the Scottish Borders in 1998; it has also opened a campus in Dubai in 2006 with another campus being built in Putrajaya, Malaysia in 2012.

Heriot-Watt's main campus is located in Riccarton in South West Edinburgh in 380 acres of beautiful parkland. Included on the campus is the student residences, a postgraduate centre, shops, several library collections, childcare,

new rooms opened as part of a £14m residences development, replacing some of the campus's older accommodation.

Heriot-Watt has a very good reputation for producing strong work prospects for its students, with 80% in graduate-level jobs six months after leaving the institution. In 2012, the National Student survey voted Heriot-Watt the most popular in Scotland and fourth in the UK; it showed the largest increase in UK applicants of any UK university for the 2013 academic session.

In 2012, Heriot-Watt was named as the Sunday Times Scottish University of the Year – with the paper emphasizing the employability of the institution›s graduates.

healthcare, a chaplaincy, a variety of recreational and sports facilities and a museum. The Edinburgh Conference Centre and Europe›s oldest research park is also on the Riccarton Campus.

Heriot-Watt's Edinburgh Campus has 1,600 furnished rooms available for students, allowing the University to guarantee accommodation to all full-time first-year undergraduates and postgraduates. In September 2012, 300

There are many famous graduates from Heriot-Watt including Adam Crozier, Chief Executive of ITV; Fiona Hyslop and Sarah Boyack, MSPs; Graham Watson, MEP; and Lord Mike Watson, Baron Watson of Invergowrie, former MP and MSP; Dame Muriel Spark, award winning Scottish novelist; and Irvine Welsh, author of Trainspotting.

QUEEN MARGARET UNIVERSITY

Queen Margaret University is a modern university located in Musselburgh, East Lothian, near Edinburgh. It is named after Saint Margaret, wife of King Malcolm III of Scotland. Christian Guthrie Wright and Louisa Stevenson who were both members of the Edinburgh Ladies' Educational Association founded Queen Margaret University in 1875, as The Edinburgh School of Cookery and Domestic Economy.

The School was founded as a women-only institution, its ambition to improve women›s access to higher education and to improve the diets of working class families. The teaching was initially delivered in lectures held at the Royal Museum; this was supplemented by a programme of public lectures and demonstrations that were delivered nationwide. However, in 1877 the School established a base at Shandwick Place, in Haymarket.

In 1891, the school moved to Atholl Crescent and expanded its

BELOW Musselburgh campus, Queen Margaret University

courses, offering residential places to students. In 1909, the School was designated a Central Institution and brought under the public control of the Scottish Education Department.

In 1961, the College purchased the Corstorphine campus and a portion of the Clermiston estate from developers. The campus was first occupied by the college in 1970, opened by Princess Alice, Duchess of Gloucester who was Patron of the institution until her death in 2004.

In 1972, the name *Queen Margaret College* was adopted to dissociate the college from the narrow field of domestic science. The college then broadened its range of courses, to include the paramedical and healthcare fields.

In 2010, the Schools of Social Sciences, Media and Communication and Drama and Creative Industries were merged with the School now offering new courses in media, film, public relations, psychology, drama and performance, costume design and production, cultural management, arts management, festival management, acting for stage and screen, social justice, and psychology and sociology.

The university has recently launched a new Master's degree in gastronomy which is the first of its kind in the UK allowing students to engage with the broad range of issues connected with food, provenance, diet, health, and nutrition. The degree encompasses the cultural, historical, and anthropological aspects of Scotland as well as the science of food, the marketplace and political and economic issues which relate to food.

The university is the first higher education institution in the east of Scotland to host the Children's University, which aims to help school children, aged between seven to fourteen years of age to become confident learners and broaden their horizons.

EDINBURGH COLLEGE OF ART

Edinburgh College of Art (ECA) is an art, design, creative and performing arts school providing higher education in art and design, architecture, history of art and music disciplines for more than 2000 University of Edinburgh students.

The college has an international reputation as one of the most successful art colleges in Europe and is mainly located in the Old Town, overlooking the Grassmarket with the Lauriston Place campus not far from the University of Edinburgh's George Square campus.

The college was founded in 1760, gaining its present name and site in 1907. It was formerly associated with Heriot-Watt University, with degrees being issued by the University of Edinburgh since 2004.

The college formally merged with the university in August 2011, and now combines the School of Arts, Culture and Environment and continues to exist with the name Edinburgh College of Art as an enlarged school in the College of Humanities and Social Science.

Notable architects who have graduated from the college include: Sir Nicholas Grimshaw, Sir Basil Urwin Spence and

ABOVE Front entrance of Edinburgh College of Arts

Sir James Duncan Dunbar-Nasmith.

While artists to graduate from college include Dame Elizabeth Violet Blackadder, John Maxwell, Patrick Reyntiens; William Crozier, Callum Innes and William MacTaggart. Great sculptors who have graduated include Alexander Carrick and Sir Eduardo Luigi Paolozzi. Several famous musicians who were past pupils include Alexander 'Sandy' Brown and the Django Django quartet of David Maclean, Vincent Neff, Jimmy Dixon and Tommy Grace.

EDINBURGH ACADEMY

Henry Cockburn and Leonard Horner, the school founders agreed in 1822 that Edinburgh required a new school to promote classical learning.

Edinburgh's Royal High School had provided a classical education but a greater provision was needed for the teaching of Greek, to compete with some of England's public schools.

Cockburn and Horner had recruited John Russell as a co-founder and the three of them put a proposal to the City Council for the building of a new school. In 1823, the City Fathers gave their approval. Fifteen Directors were elected, including the three founders and 12 other luminaries, including Sir Walter Scott, Sir John Hay and Robert Dundas.

The famous ex-pupils from the Edinburgh Academy include Robert Louis Stevenson celebrated author; James Hall Nasmyth, Inventor of the Steam Hammer; Magnus Magnusson, television presenter; and Admiral of the Fleet, Andrew Cunningham, victor of Taranto and Matapan battles during the Second World War.

ROYAL HIGH SCHOOL, EDINBURGH

The Royal High School of Edinburgh is a co-educational state school administered by the City of Edinburgh Council. The school was founded in 1128 and is one of the oldest schools in Scotland.

The RHS's national profile has given it a flagship role in education piloting such experiments as the introduction of the Certificate of Secondary Education and the curricular integration of European Studies and the International Baccalaureate.

The RHS is the 18th-oldest school in the world and has a history of almost 900 years. Historians have associated its origins with the beginning of the 12th century renaissance. The school first entered the historical record as the seminary of Holyrood Abbey, founded for Alwin and the Augustinian canons by David I in 1128.

In 1505, the school became the first in Britain to be designated a high school and in 1566, following the Reformation, Mary, Queen of Scots, transferred the school from the control of Holyrood Abbey to Edinburgh Town Council. From 1590 James VI accorded it royal patronage as the *Schola Regia Edimburgensis*.

The romantic era at the turn of the 19th century was for Scotland a famous age of literature and won the Royal High School an international reputation which resulted in an increase of foreign students, among them French royalty. The RHS was used as a model

for the first public high school in the United States, the English High School of Boston, in 1821.

There is a large list of notable former pupils including such luminaries as Alexander Graham Bell (1847–1922), inventor of the telephone; and Ronnie Corbett (born 1930), the diminutive entertainer who was half of The Two Ronnies comedy act with Ronnie Barker.

ABOVE A vintage photograph of interior of the Royal High School Hall at Regent Road

FETTES COLLEGE

Sir William Fettes (1750–1836), a former Lord Provost of Edinburgh and wealthy city merchant, bequeathed the sum of £166,000 to be set aside for the education of poor children and orphans of the city to commemorate the death of his son William.

In 1870, the bequest was affected and invested and the accumulated sum was then used to acquire the land and to build the main building. Fettes College opened with 53 pupils (40 were Foundation Scholars with 11 others boarding and 2 day pupils).

Famously, the school came into disrepute when Anthony Chenevix-Trench (1971–79), formerly of Eton took over as Headmaster. The investigative journalist Paul Foot wrote an exposé in *Private Eye* detailing his excessive use of corporal punishment while he was a Housemaster at Shrewsbury School.

The school was placed fourth by the Daily Telegraph league table of schools in 1998 and was placed fifth by the Sunday Times in 1999 in the list of top mixed schools in the UK. In 2001, the Sunday Times declared Fettes the "Scottish School of the Year."

Notable Old Fettesians include Frank Barnwell, Chief designer of the Bristol bomber; and Tony Blair, Prime Minister of the UK.

MERCHISTON CASTLE SCHOOL

In May 1833, Charles Chalmers leased Merchiston Castle (the former home of John Napier, the inventor of logarithms), which at that time stood in rural surroundings, to open his academy, starting with just 30 boys.

Over time, the number of pupils grew and the Merchiston Castle became too small to accommodate the school. So in 1930, the governors decided to move the school to Colinton House, four miles south-west of Edinburgh in Colinton.

Three years later, in 1933, Merchiston celebrated its centenary which was attended by the Duke and Duchess of York. Fifty years on, in 1983, at a time of further expansion and with 350 boys on the roll, their daughter, the now Queen Elizabeth II, visited the school for its 150th anniversary.

Notable former pupils and staff include Air Marshal Sir John Baird, Surgeon General UK Armed Forces 1997-2000; Sir James Marjoribanks, career diplomat who presented Britain›s successful application to join the EU in 1967; William Lovat Fraser, international cricketer and rugby union footballer; and Sir Peter Burt- Governor & Chief Executive of Bank of Scotland

BELOW Merchiston Castle School

from 1996 to 2001, and Former Chairman of ITV.

Merchiston has produced international rugby union footballers for Scotland, Ireland and England. These include Roger Baird, Iain Fullarton, Phil Godman, Duncan Hodge, John Jeffrey, Craig Joiner, Jamie Mayer, William Neilson, Thomas Anderson and Peter Walton.

GEORGE HERIOT'S SCHOOL

George Heriot's School is currently one of the leading Scottish independent primary and secondary schools. It is located on Lauriston Place in the Old Town of Edinburgh and has more than 1600 pupils, 155 teaching staff and 80 non-teaching staff.

The school is recognised as one of the leading schools in the UK in terms of academic results, extra-curricular provision and bursarial and foundation support.

The main building of the school is famous for its renaissance architecture, which is the work of William Wallace. It was also the first large building to be constructed outside the Edinburgh city walls, next to Greyfriars Kirk, in 1620, in open grounds, overlooked by the Castle directly to the north.

On his death in 1624, George Heriot left around £25,000 Scottish Pounds, the equivalent to several tens of millions today – to found a 'hospital' the then name for this kind of charitable school to care for the "poor, fatherless children" of Edinburgh.

The construction of Heriot's Hospital (as it was first called) started in 1628, just outside the city walls of Edinburgh. On its completion, it was occupied by Oliver Cromwell›s English forces during the invasion of Scotland during the Third English Civil War; the building was used as a barracks, with horses stabled in the chapel.

In 1659, the hospital opened with 30 sickly children in residence. When its finances grew, the school took in other pupils in addition to the orphans for whom it was intended. In the 1880s, it began to charge fees. However, to this day it serves its charitable objective, providing free education to fatherless children, which are referred to in Edinburgh as 'foundationers'.

The school founded ten 'free schools' in Edinburgh in 1837, educating several thousand pupils across the city, which were sadly closed in 1885. One of them, with a copy of several of the features of the original Lauriston Place building, is at the east end of the Cowgate and is now serving as a Salvation Army hostel.

The school has many famous graduates including Hippolyte Blanc (1844 - 1917), architect; Henry Raeburn (1756 - 1823), painter; Hyman Levy (1889 - 1975), Scottish philosopher; Stephen Woolman, Lord Woolman, Senator of the College of Justice; and Nick Abbot, talk radio presenter.

BELOW The Quadrangle, Heriot's Hospital

Chapter 8

Famous Sons and Daughters

Edinburgh has been home to many great thinkers, scientists, musicians, actors, writers and inventors. These are just some of the more famous sons and daughters of the city:

ARCHITECTS:

HIPPOLYTE BLANC

Hippolyte Blanc was born at 37 North Frederick Street in Edinburgh; he was the third son of four children, to French parents who ran a business on George Street importing and manufacturing ladies shoes. Blanc went to George Heriot's School, winning the dux medal in 1859, and was then articled to the architect David Rhind. In 1864, after completing his articles, he joined the Government Office of Works under Robert Matheson, where he became a senior draughtsman in 1869.

Blanc designed many church buildings including Kirkliston Free Church (1880); St Luke's, Broughty Ferry (1884); Coats Memorial Baptist Church, Paisley (1885); and Morningside Free Church, Edinburgh (1892) which is now the Church Hill Theatre. He carried out restoration work to Edinburgh Castle (1886); John Knox House (1886); St Cuthbert's Church (1892); and St Duthac's Church, Tain (1896).

Secular work includes Mayville Gardens in Trinity, Edinburgh (1881), a pleasant and quirky Victorian cul-de-sac with a low terrace of ornate houses on each side. Other major commissions included houses at Eriska, Argyll, and Ferguslie

Park, Paisley (1888–91), since demolished.

In 1871 Blanc was elected president of the Edinburgh Architectural Association for the first of three times. He became a fellow of the Society of Antiquaries of Scotland in 1879, a fellow of the Royal Institute of British Architects (RIBA) in 1901, and was elected to the Royal Scottish Academy (RSA) in 1896.

In addition, he was an active member of several other learned societies. He wrote and lectured extensively, largely on the subject of medieval church architecture. Blanc served as president and treasurer of the RSA from 1907–17, and was president of the Edinburgh Photographic Society from 1888 until 1892, and honorary president from 1896 until his death.

SIR WILLIAM BRUCE OF KINROSS

Sir William Bruce of Kinross, 1st Baronet (c. 1630 – 1 January 1710) was a Scottish gentleman-architect, know as the effective founder of classical architecture in Scottish History.

Sir William was a key figure in introducing the Palladian style into Scotland and has been compared to the pioneering English architects such as Indigo

ABOVE
Sir William Bruce

Jones and Christopher Wren and to the other introducers of French style in English domestic architecture such as Hugh May and Sir Roger Pratt.

Sir William Bruce was a merchant in Rotterdam during the 1650s, playing a key role in the Restoration of King Charles II in 1659 by carrying messages between the exiled king and General Monck.

His loyalty to the king was rewarded with lucrative official appointments including that of Surveyor General of the King's Works in Scotland, effectively making Bruce the "king's architect".

His patrons included John Maitland, 1st Duke of Lauderdale who was the most powerful man in Scotland at that time. Sir William Bruce rose to become a member of parliament, and briefly sat on the Scottish Privy Council.

Despite his lack of technical expertise, Bruce became the most prominent architect of his time in Scotland. Beginning in the 1660s, Bruce built and remodelled a number of country houses, including Thirlestane Castle for the Duke of Lauderdale, and Prestonfield House.

Among his most significant work was his own Palladian mansion at Kinross, which was built on the Loch Leven estate, after he had purchased it in 1675. As the king's architect he undertook the rebuilding of the Royal Palace of Holyroodhouse in the 1670s, which gave the palace its present appearance.

After the death of Charles II, Bruce lost political favour, and later, following the accession of William and Mary, he was imprisoned more than once as a suspected Jacobite. However, he managed to continue his architectural work, often providing his services to others with Jacobite sympathies.

SIR ROBERT STODART LORIMER

Lorimer was born in Edinburgh, the son of James Lorimer, who was Regius Professor of Public Law at Edinburgh University from 1862 to 1890. He was educated at Edinburgh Academy and later at Edinburgh University.

He was part of a gifted family, being the younger brother of painter John Henry Lorimer, and father to the sculptor Hew Lorimer. In 1878 the Lorimer family acquired the lease of Kellie Castle in Fife and began its restoration for use as a holiday home.

He was influenced by Scottish domestic architecture of the 16th and 17th centuries and the Scots Baronial style of Kellie Castle where he had spent much time as a young man. From his time in Bodley's office, Lorimer was influenced by the ideas of William Morris, and went on to become a committed exponent of the Arts and Crafts approach to architecture.

He assembled a collaborative group of artists and craftsmen who, collectively, often contributed to his various commissions and to the manufacture of furniture sent to the Arts and Crafts exhibitions in London. In 1896 he was elected to the Art Workers Guild.

The outbreak of World War I restricted the demand for large new houses and his attention shifted to smaller scale projects, war memorials, and restorations.

He already had a reputation as one of Scotland's leading restoration architects following the restoration of Earlshall and Dunderave, and he went on to carry out significant alteration and restoration works at Dunrobin Castle in Sutherland following a fire in 1915, and at Balmanno Castle in Perthshire, in 1916, said to have been the only one of his commissions he would like to have lived in.

Although much of his work, and reputation, was in the sphere of domestic architecture, Lorimer also carried out significant public works. Principal amongst these include his design for the new chapel for the Knights of the Thistle in St Giles' Cathedral, Edinburgh, in 1911. He received a knighthood for his efforts and went on to gain the commission for the Scottish National War Memorial at Edinburgh Castle in 1919, subsequently opened by the Prince of Wales in 1927.

Lorimer became President of the professional body in Scotland, the Incorporation of Architects in Scotland, and it was during his tenure in office that the body received its second royal charter, permitting use of the term 'Royal' in the title. Lorimer was a fellow of the North British Academy of Arts. He died in Edinburgh in 1929.

BELOW Robert Lorimer at work in the office of Sir Robert Rowand Anderson. Painted by his elder brother John Henry Lorimer, 1886

FAMOUS SONS AND DAUGHTERS

WILLIAM WALLACE

From 1615, Wallace is known to have been the leading mason working on the King's Lodgings at Edinburgh Castle. On 18 April 1617 he was appointed King's Master Mason, holding this post until his death.

Wallace was commissioned in 1618 to rebuild the north range of Linlithgow Palace, which had collapsed in 1605. He was responsible for design as well as building, and executed the new range in an Anglo-Flemish style, which he helped to popularise in Scotland.

This was followed with works to Winton House, near Pencaitland, for George Seton, 3rd Earl of Winton, which he undertook from 1620 to 1627. In 1621 he was made a burgess of Edinburgh, and later served as Deacon of the Edinburgh Masons Lodge.

From 1628 until his death Wallace was engaged on the design and construction of Heriot's Hospital, now a school, again in the Anglo-Flemish style. He was almost certainly the principal designer of the building, which was continued after his death by William Aytoun.

One of Wallace's last works was carving the monument to John Byres of Coates in Greyfriars' Kirkyard, unpaid for at his death, and his will also includes debts for works at Moray House.

MEDICINE, SCIENCE AND ENGINEERING:

CHARLES BELL

Charles Bell was born in Edinburgh in November 1774 and attended Edinburgh High School and Edinburgh University where he took his medical degree in 1798. He was soon admitted to the

which had a profound influence on Alexander Graham Bell's life's works.

Bell was educated at Edinburgh's Royal High School; he left with an undistinguished record and poor grades. However he returned to attend the University of Edinburgh before moving to Canada. He is famous for transmitting speech via a simple receiver that put electricity into sound. In 1876 he was granted a patent for the telephone which made him a very wealthy man.

Royal College of Surgeons in Edinburgh, teaching anatomy and operating. Here he published two volumes of books on anatomy and dissection.

Charles Bell is noted for discovering the difference between sensory nerves and motor nerves and spinal cord and also for the first description of Bell's palsy.

ALEXANDER GRAHAM BELL

Alexander Graham Bell was born in Edinburgh on March 3, 1847. His father, grandfather and brother were all associated with work on elocution and speech; his mother and his wife were both deaf,

ANDREW BALFOUR

Andrew Balfour was educated at the University of St Andrews, where he was mentored by his brother James, and studied philosophy and arithmetic under Thomas Glegg. Graduating with an MA, he moved to London and in 1650, became a pupil to John Wedderburn, the King's physician.

He travelled in France, studying in Paris and at the University of Caen, where he gained a degree with a dissertation entitled De Venae Sectione in Dysenteria. As a student he spent much time with his friend Sir Robert Sibbald, the two travelling together and studying together. Returning to London, he became a governor to John Wilmot, Earl of Rochester, travelling to Italy with him in 1667.

In 1667 Balfour set up medical practice in St Andrews. By this time he had amassed a large collection of scientific and medical books, curiosities and instruments: his 'rarities' were called the 'Museaum Balfourianum' by contemporaries.

In 1670 he moved to set up practice in Edinburgh. He planted a small botanical garden next to his house. He became a friend of Robert Sibbald, whom he succeeded as third president of the College of Physicians in 1684. Balfour and Sibbald set up a garden together near Holyrood Abbey, which Balfour subsequently persuaded the university to fund.

DUNCAN NAPIER

Duncan Napier was a Victorian botanist and herbalist. His early start in life was hard as he was orphaned at an early age. From his youth he was fascinated by plants and nature.

His interest in herbal medicine started when he found a book about it on an Edinburgh market stall. He had been apprenticed to a baker and, possibly due to

the flour dust, had developed a chronic cough. After reading the book's recipes he experimented and made a Lobelia Cough Syrup that cleared up his cough within six months.

Encouraged by this success, Duncan started to make other herbal medicines and try them out on his friends and family, collecting herbs from the surrounding areas of Edinburgh in the Pentland Hills.

He became a member of the Edinburgh Botanical Society and was encouraged by his contemporaries to open a herbal shop. Duncan Napier opened his first herbal shop on Bristo Place, Edinburgh in May 1860, so that the local community could benefit from herbal medicine. The shop and clinic at Bristo Place remains open to this day and is now Scotland's oldest and only remaining herbal house.

Napier collected herbs and plants from Edinburgh and the Borders, often rising before dawn and returning in time to open his shop to the waiting queue of people. Bunches of herbs were dried in the basement to be made into syrups, tinctures and ointments.

Some of these formula are still manufactured today. Family holidays were spent with his sons walking the Highlands of Scotland and collecting plants and herbs. His sons went into the business with him and it became D. Napier and Sons.

In the mid-19th century, British herbalists banded together into the National Association, which became the National Institute of Medical Herbalists. This is still the oldest and major professional organisation for herbal practitioners in the UK, with members being recognised worldwide. Napier was a founder member.

When Napier died at the age of 91, the shop was taken over by his son and the business remained in the family for many years passing down through the generations. The last family member to carry on the practice was John Napier, a member of the National Institute of Medical Herbalists.

MILITARY:

DOUGLAS FORD (GC)

Captain Douglas Ford (1918-1943) was a Royal Scots officer and British prisoner of war in World War II, who was posthumously awarded the George Cross for conspicuous gallantry.

Ford was born in Galashiels in September, 1918. He was a son of Mr. and Mrs. Douglas Ford, of 25 Bryce Avenue, Portobello. He was educated at the Royal High School in Edinburgh. A keen sportsman, excelling in rugby and cricket, he rose to school captain in 1936.

He was 20, and on part-time studies at Edinburgh University for chartered accountancy, when he joined the Royal Scots at the outbreak of war. A member of the university O.T.C., he was commissioned, and posted to Hong Kong.

Ford was still serving in the 2nd Battalion, Royal Scots, when he and his brother were taken prisoner by the invading Japanese upon the fall of Hong Kong in December 1941. During his captivity at Sham Shui Po POW camp he made contact with British agents and planned, in conjunction with other officers, a major break out.

Before the plans could be put into operation the Japanese grew suspi-

FAMOUS SONS AND DAUGHTERS

cious and interrogated him and others they suspected of involvement. Despite torture in Stanley Prison, starvation and a sentence of death he refused to betray his comrades.

After being forced to dig his own grave he was executed by Japanese firing squad, at Big Wave Bay on the 18th of December 1943. He is buried in Stanley Prison cemetery.

SANDY HODGE (ROYAL NAVY OFFICER)

Captain Alexander Mitchell ("Sandy") Hodge, GC, VRD, DL RNVR (1916–1997) was a recipient of the Empire Gallantry Medal which was later exchanged for the George Cross.

Sandy Hodge was born on 23 June 1916 at Blairgowrie in Scotland. He was educated at Fettes College and Edinburgh University and joined the Royal Navy Volunteer Reserve in 1938.

He was awarded the Empire Gallantry Medal for bravery while a sublieutenant during a naval action on 14 March 1940 when a bomb exploded in a bomb room on HMS Eagle leaving 13 people dead and one injured: he played a major role in the rescue.

After the war he became senior partner of Cowan & Stewart, a firm of lawyers. He also became chairman of Standard Life. He also served as Deputy Lieutenant of Edinburgh.

ARTS:

RORY BREMNER

Rory Bremner is a Scottish impression-ist and comedian, famous for his work in political satire and impressions of British public figures. He was born in Edinburgh and educated at Clifton Hall School in Newbridge, a suburb of the city. He recently presented a one-off show for BBC Scotland which takes a satirical look at Scottish politics and the independence referendum.

SEAN CONNERY

Sean Connery was born in Fountain Bridge, Edinburgh; his mother was a cleaning woman and his father, Jo-seph Connery a factory worker and lorry driver. Connery is famous for portraying the character James Bond and starred in seven Bond films. He has 12 BAFTA awards, an Academy Award and three Golden Globes. In July 2000, he received a knighthood. He is a member of the Scottish Na-tional party and has stated that he will never return to live in Scotland until it becomes an independent state.

SIR ARTHUR IGNATIUS CONAN DOYLE

Sir Arthur Conan Doyle was born 22nd May 1859 at 11 Picardy Place in Edinburgh. He went on to study medicine at the University of Edinburgh Medical School and became famous for his fictional stories about the detective Sherlock Holmes. His other works include fantasy, science fiction stories, plays, romances and historical novels.

ABOVE
Ronnie Corbett

RIGHT
Sir Arthur Ignatius
Conan Doyle

OPPOSITE
Ian Rankin signing
his Dark Entries
Hellblazer graphic
novel in the
Edinburgh branch
of Forbidden Planet
International

RONNIE CORBETT CBE

Ronnie Corbett is a Scottish actor and comedian famous for his long association with Ronnie Barker in the television comedy series the Two Ronnies. He was born in Edinburgh in 1930, attending the Royal High School. Ronnie Corbett has starred in many famous sitcoms and films, including the thriller comedy Burke and Hare in February 2010. He was appointed Commander of the Order of the British Empire in the 2012 New Years Honours lists for services to entertainment and charity.

ALEXANDER MCCALL SMITH

Alexander McCall Smith was born in Bulawayo but returned to study law at the University of Edinburgh. He returned to Africa and taught law at the University of Botswana. He now lives with his wife Elizabeth in Edinburgh. Alexander McCall Smith has gained worldwide fame for creating the book series, The No 1 Ladies Detective Agency.

IAN RANKIN

Ian Rankin OBE is a Scottish crime writer, famous for his Inspector Rebus novels. He attended the University of Edinburgh and remained after graduation to work on his doctorate, also teaching at the University. Rankin's famous Inspector Rebus novels are set mainly in Edinburgh; ten of these novels have now been adapted for television. Rankin now lives in Edinburgh with his wife Miranda and two sons.

MURIEL SPARK

Dame Muriel Spark DBE was born in Edinburgh and educated at Herriot Watt College. She became an award-winning

JK ROWLING

JK Rowling is best known as the author of the multi-million selling children's fantasy series featuring wizard Harry Potter. The Potter books have gained worldwide fame, winning multiple awards and selling more than 400 million copies. They are the biggest-selling book series in history and have become the highest grossing film series in history as well. The majority of the Harry Potter books were written in Edinburgh in the Elephant House, a gourmet tea and coffee house overlooking Edinburgh Castle.

ROBERT LOUIS STEVENSON

Robert Louis Stevenson was born in Edinburgh at 8 Howard Place on the 13th of November 1850. He was educated at the Edinburgh Academy and also studied engineering at the University of Edinburgh. Stevenson went on to become one of Scotland's most famous novelists. His books include Treasure Island, Kidnapped and the Strange Case of Dr Jekyll and Mr Hyde.

ABOVE
Author J.K. Rowling

Scottish novelist, the Times newspaper naming her in its list of 50 greatest British writers since 1945. Her most famous book, The Prime of Miss Jean Brodie received huge critical acclaim and she has twice been shortlisted for the Booker prize, in 1969 for The Public Image and in 1981 for Loitering with Intent.

IRVINE WELSH

Irvine Welsh was born in the area of Leith in Edinburgh in September 1958. He was educated in Muirhouse and left Edinburgh for London, returning to study for an MBA at Herriot Watt University. Welsh is a notable Scottish novelist and playwright, with his best-known novel Trainspotting, depicting the brutality of Edinburgh life, and being made into a blockbuster movie starring Ewan MacCregor.

LEFT
Robert Louis Stevenson

ABOVE
Irvine Welsh

SPORTS:

GAVIN HASTINGS OBE

Gavin Hastings, who was born in Edinburgh, is a famous Scotland rugby union player who won 61 caps for Scotland, 20 as captain, and is considered to be one of the best rugby players to come out of Scotland.

'Big Gav' played fullback and captained the British & Irish Lions on their tour to New Zealand in 1993 (after playing in all three tests in the 1989 tour to Australia).

Former national coach Ian McGeechan said of him: " Gavin is a big man in every sense of the word ... his greatest asset was to engender confidence in those around him and to lead by example when the opposition had to be taken on. In New Zealand, they considered him simply the best full-back in the world."

CHRIS HOY

Sir Christopher Andrew Hoy was born in March 1976 and grew up in the west of Edinburgh. He was educated at George Watson's Col-

lege in Edinburgh transferring from the University of St Andrews to the University of Edinburgh graduating with a B.Sc. Honours in Applied Sports Science. His claim to fame though is as a cyclist, as he is a six time Olympic champion, winning a total of seven Olympic Games medals, six gold and one silver. He is the 11 times world champion and the most successful Olympic cyclist ever.

GRAEME SOUNESS

Graeme Souness was born in May 1953 in Edinburgh. He was not only a very successful and famous football player who won numerous leagues and cups with Liverpool but became a very successful manager with Liverpool, Galatasaray, Southampton and Newcastle United. He is now an astute media pundit and is a regular fixture on Sky Sports television.

SCOTTISH ENLIGHTENMENT FIGURES:

JOSEPH BLACK

Joseph Black FRSE FRCPE FPSG (16 April 1728 – 6 December 1799) was a Scottish physician and chemist, known for his discoveries of latent heat, specific heat, and carbon dioxide. He was Professor of Anatomy and Chemistry at the University of Glasgow for 10 years from 1756, and then Professor of Medicine and Chemistry at the University of Edinburgh from 1766, teaching and lecturing there for more than 30 years. The chemistry buildings at both the University of Edinburgh and the University of Glasgow are named after Black.

In about 1750, while still a student, Black developed the analytical balance based on a lightweight beam balanced on a wedge-shaped fulcrum. Each arm carried a pan on which the sample or standard weights was placed. It far exceeded the accuracy of any other balance of the time and became an important scientific instrument in most chemistry laboratories.

Black was a member of the Poker Club and associated with David Hume, Adam Smith, and the literati of the Scottish Enlightenment. Black never married. He died peacefully at his home in Edinburgh in 1799 at the age of 71 and is buried in Greyfriars Kirkyard. In 2011 scientific equipment believed to belong to Black was discovered during an archaeological dig at the University of Edinburgh.

JAMES HUTTON

James Hutton FRSE was a Scottish geologist, physician, chemical manufacturer, naturalist, and experimental agriculturalist. He originated the theory of uniformitarianism - a fundamental principle of geology which explains the features of the Earth's crust by means of natural processes over geologic time. Hutton's work established geology as a proper science, and thus he is often referred to as the "Father of Modern Geology".

He was born in Edinburgh on 3 June 1726 as one of five children of William Hutton, a merchant who was Edinburgh City Treasurer, but who died in 1729 when James was still young. Hutton's mother - Sarah Balfour - insisted on his education at the High School of Edinburgh where he was particularly interested in mathematics and chemistry.

When he was 14 he attended the University of Edinburgh as a "student of humanity" i.e. Classics (Latin and Greek). He was apprenticed to the lawyer George Chalmers WS when he was 17, but took more interest in chemical experiments than legal work.

At the age of 18, he became a physician's assistant, and attended lectures in medicine at the University of Edinburgh. After three years he went to the University of Paris to continue his studies, taking the degree of Doctor of Medicine at Leiden University in 1749.

After his degree Hutton returned to London, then in mid-1750 went back to Edinburgh and resumed chemical experiments with close friend, James Davie. Hutton owned and rented out properties in Edinburgh, employing a factor to manage this business.

He had a house built in 1770 at St John's Hill, Edinburgh, overlooking Salisbury Crags. This later became the Balfour family home and, in 1840, the birthplace of the psychiatrist James Crichton-Browne.

Hutton was one of the most influential participants in the Scottish En-

lightenment, and fell in with numerous first-class minds in the sciences including John Playfair, philosopher David Hume and economist Adam Smith.

Hutton held no position in Edinburgh University and communicated his scientific findings through the Royal Society of Edinburgh. He was particularly friendly with Joseph Black, and the two of them together with Adam Smith founded the Oyster Club for weekly meetings, with Hutton and Black finding a venue which turned out to have rather disreputable associations.

Chapter 9

Sport

Whilst Edinburgh is probably best known as the capital city of history, culture and finance, it is also a hotbed of sporting activity both professionally and on an amateur level.

The city boasts two professional football clubs: Heart of Midlothian, founded in 1874, and Hibernian, founded just a year later in 1875.

Known locally as 'Hearts' and 'Hibs', they are the oldest city rivals in Scotland, and the Edinburgh derby is one of the oldest derby matches in world football.

Hearts are based in Gorgie, in the west of the city, having been formed by a group of friends from the Heart of Midlothian Dancing Club!

The modern club crest is based on the Heart of Midlothian mosaic on the city's Royal Mile and the team's colours are predominantly maroon and white.

Hearts play at Tynecastle Stadium where home matches have been played since 1886. After renovating the ground into an all-seater stadium following the findings of the Taylor Report in 1990, the original capacity of 18,000 has been reduced to roughly 17,000 in order to comply with UEFA regulations.

Hearts have won the Scottish League championship four times, most recently in 1959-60, when they also retained the Scottish League Cup to complete a league and cup double – the only club outside of the Old Firm of Celtic and Rangers to achieve the feat.

The club's famous 1957-58 league winning side, led up front by Jimmy Wardhaugh, Willie Bauld and Alfie Con Sr. (who were affectionately known as *The Terrible Trio*) set the record for the number of goals scored in a league campaign (132) and became the only side to finish a season with a goal difference exceeding 100.

Hearts have won the Scottish Cup eight times, most recently in 2012 after a 5–1 demolition of city-rivals Hibernian; and the League Cup four times, most recently in 1962 after a 1–0 victory against

Kilmarnock. Their most recent Scottish League Cup Final appearance was in 2013 when they lost to St Mirren 3–2, despite a brace of goals from Ryan Stevenson.

In 1958, Hearts became the third

LEFT Heart Of Midlothian mosaic

ABOVE the Scottish Cup is the oldest national trophy in world football

Scottish and fifth British team to compete in Europe. The club reached the quarter finals of the 1988-89 UEFA Cup, narrowly losing out to Bayern Munich 2–1 on aggregate. More recently, Hearts became both the first Scottish side and the first British side to reach the UEFA Cup (now Europa League) group stage in its inaugural 2004 season. Hearts were also the first non-Old Firm team to reach the qualification stages of the Champions League in 2006.

Sadly, the club is currently in administration (and were deducted league points because of it which resulted in their relegation at the end of the 2013/14 season) bringing to an end the controversial reign of owner Vladimir Romanov who had been the majority shareholder since 2005.

Hibs, based in Leith in the north of Edinburgh, was founded by Irish immigrants but support for the club is now based on geography rather than ethnicity or religion. The Irish heritage of Hibs is still reflected, however, in its name, green coloured shirts and badge.

Home matches have been played at the Easter Road stadium since 1893 when the club joined the Scottish Football League. Hibs had played in the top of the league system since 1999 but under manager Terry Butcher (a former England captain) were relegated at the end of the 2013-14 season. Butcher has since been sacked.

The team has won the league championships four times, most recently in 1952. Three of those four championships were won between 1948 and 1952, when the club had the services of 'The Famous Five' – Gordon Smith, Bobby Johnstone, Lawrie Reilly, Eddie Turnbull and Willie Ormond - arguably the strongest forward line in the history of Scottish football.

The club has won the Scottish Cup twice, in 1887 and 1902, but has lost ten finals since, most recently in 2013. The last major trophy won by the club was the 2007 League Cup when Kilmarnock were beaten 5–1 in the final. It was the third time Hibs had won the League Cup, also winning in 1972 and 1991.

Edinburgh was also home to four other Scottish football league cubs: Edinburgh City; Leith Athletic; St. Bernard's and Meadowbank Thistle, who played at Meadowbank until 1995, when the club moved to Livingston and became Livingston FC.

The Scottish national football team has

ABOVE
Murrayfield Stadium

very occasionally played at Easter Road and Tynecastle although its normal home stadium is Hampden Park in Glasgow.

The Scotland national rugby team, however, and the professional Edinburgh team play at the city's Murrayfield Stadium which is owned by the Scottish Rugby Union and is also used for other events, including music concerts. It is the largest capacity stadium in Scotland, seating 67,130 spectators.

The national team takes part in the annual Six Nations Championship and participates in the Rugby World Cup, which takes place every four years and is to be played in England & Wales in 2015.

The Scottish rugby team dates back to 1871, where they beat England in the first international rugby union match at Raeburn Place. Scotland competed in the Five Nations from the inaugural tournament in 1883, winning it 14 times outright—including the last ever Five Nations in 1999 and sharing it another eight times.

In 2000 the competition accepted a sixth competitor, Italy, thereby creating the Six Nations tournament. Scotland has yet to win the competition since then. The Rugby World Cup was introduced in 1987 and Scotland has competed in all seven competitions, the most recent being in 2011. Scotland's best finish came

ABOVE Easter Road stadium

in 1991, where they lost to the All Blacks in the third-place play-off.

Scotland, not surprisingly, has a strong rivalry with the English national team. They both annually compete for the Calcutta Cup as part of the Six Nations. England are the current holders after defeating Scotland 13–6 at Murrayfield in the 2012 Six Nations maintaining it in the 2013 and 2014 championship.

Edinburgh is also home to RBS Premier One rugby teams Heriot's Rugby Club, Boroughmuir RFC, the Edinburgh Academicals and Currie RFC.

Rugby League is represented by the Edinburgh Eagles who play in the Rugby

BELOW The Grange
cricket club, home
of the Scotland
Cricket team

League Conference Scotland Division. Murrayfield Stadium has hosted the Magic Weekend where all Super League matches are played in the stadium over one weekend.

The Scottish cricket team, which represents Scotland internationally and in the Friends Provident Trophy, plays their home matches at the Grange cricket club in the Stockbridge district of Edinburgh.

The Edinburgh Capitals are the latest of a succession of ice hockey clubs in the Scottish capital. Previously Edinburgh was represented by the Murrayfield Racers and the Edinburgh Racers. The club plays their home games at the Murrayfield Ice Rink and has competed in the ten-team professional Elite Ice Hockey League since the 2005–06 season.

The Edinburgh Diamond Devils is a baseball club, which won its first Scottish Championship in 1991 as the "Reivers." .The team repeated the achievement in the following year, becoming the first team to do so in league history. The same year saw the start of their first youth team, the Blue Jays. The club adopted its present name in 1999.

Edinburgh has also hosted national and international sports events including the World Student Games, the 1970 and 1986 British Commonwealth Games and the inaugural 2000 Commonwealth Youth Games. For the 1970 Games the city built Olympic standard venues and facilities including Meadowbank Stadium and the Royal Commonwealth Pool, which underwent refurbishment in 2012 and hosted the Diving competition in the 2014 Commonwealth Games, which was hosted by Glasgow.

In American Football, the Scottish Claymores played WLAF/NFL Europe games at Murrayfield including their World Bowl 96 victory. From 1995 to 1997 they played all their games there, while from 1998 to 2000 they split their home matches between Murrayfield and Glasgow's Hampden Park, then moved to Glasgow full-time, with one final Murrayfield appearance in 2002. The city's most successful non-professional team is the Edinburgh Wolves who play at Meadowbank Stadium.

The Edinburgh Marathon has been held annually in the city since 2003 with more than 16,000 runners taking part each year. Its organisers have called it "the fastest marathon in the UK" due to the elevation drop of 40 metres (130 ft.). The city also organises a half-marathon, as well as 10 km (3.1 miles) and 5km (3.1 mi) races, and hosts a traditional 5 km race on 1 January each year.

Edinburgh has a speedway team, the Edinburgh Monarchs which, since the loss of its stadium in the city, has raced at the Lothian Arena in Armadale, West Lothian. The Monarchs have won the Premier League championship three times in their history, in 2003 and again in 2008 and 2010.

BELOW Edinburgh Monarchs meeting May 2014

For sports fans and participants, the country's capital boasts an impressive array of activities to keep the locals entertained and fit.

Chapter 10

Quiz

1. **Which of these is the Queen's official residence in Scotland?**

A. Edinburgh Castle
B. Holyrood House
C. Balmoral Castle
D. Buckingham Palace

2. **What is the name of Edinburgh's main railway station?**

A. Walter Scott
B. St. Giles
C. Waverley
D. Stazione Termini

3. **Who was Robert Louis Stevenson?**

A. A gravedigger
B. A famous writer
C. A pop singer
D. A notorious doctor

4. **What is the name of the street running from Edinburgh Castle to the Palace of Holyrood House?**

A. The Royal Mile
B. Princes Street
C. Grassmarket
D. Cowgate

5. **What is the name of Edinburgh's famous Rugby stadium?**

A. Twickenham
B. Murrayfield
C. Stade de France
D. Millennium Stadium

6. **The internationally famous Edinburgh Festival always starts in which month?**

A. May
B. June
C. July
D. August

7. **Who were Burke and Hare?**

A. Famous historians
B. Architects
C. Fast-running idiots
D. Body snatchers

8. **The Patrick Geddes steps run from Johnston Terrace to the Wildlife Garden below. Who was Patrick Geddes?**

A. An environmentalist and town planner
B. A soldier who held Edinburgh Castle for Mary, Queen of Scots
C. A teacher in Castle Hill School
D. An explorer

9. **Which is Edinburgh's oldest building?**

A. St. Margaret's Chapel
B. Holyrood Palace
C. John Knox House
D. Waverley Station

10. **Sean Connery grew up in?**

A. Corstorphine
B. Fountainbridge
C. Granton
D. Bond Street

11. **What was the Edinburgh landmark known as the "Mound?"**

A. A gigantic pile of rubbish
B. The foundation for one of Britain's oldest financial institutions
C. The most direct link between the Old and New Towns
D. The Mound is all of these things

12. **Some elder Edinburgh churchyards have prominent watchtowers looking over them. What were these towers built to protect against?**

A. Desecration of gravestones by militant religious dissenters.
B. The theft of newly buried corpses for sale to anatomy teachers.
C. Invaders from England.
D. The robbery of valuables buried with the bodies of the rich

13. **Which famous author studied medicine in Edinburgh and later used the forensic knowledge acquired there to create one of literature's more famous detectives?**

A. Sir Arthur Conan Doyle
B. Agatha Christie
C. Georges Simenon
D. G. K. Chesterton

14. **An Edinburgh university, founded in 1821, is named for which two Scottish notables?**

A. James Astley and David Ainslie
B. John Napier and Queen Margaret
C. Daniel Stewart and Thomas Melville
D. George Heriot and James Watt

15. Whose gravestone in the Canongate Kirk churchyard inspired one of Charles Dickens's most notable characters?

A. Mr. Beadle Bumble
B. Wilkins McCawber
C. David Copperfield
D. Ebenezer Scrooge

16. The Royal Edinburgh Military Tattoo and the Edinburgh Festival Fringe are both elements of which larger event?

A. Edinburgh Arts
B. Edinburgh Carnival
C. Edinburgh Season
D. Edinburgh Festival

17. The first Edinburgh festival was held in?

A. 1847
B. 1874
C. 1947
D. 1974

18. Where did J.K. Rowling write the majority of her Harry Potter books?

A. The Elephant house
B. The Monkey house
C. The State house
D. The Coffee house

19. What is Arthur's Seat?

A. A Royal chair
B. A bench for Scottish parliament members
C. The main peak in Holyrood Park
D. A seating area in Edinburgh Castle

20. How long is the Royal Mile?

A. One mile
B. One and a half miles
C. One mile and 107 yards
D. One mile and 17 yards

21. What are the Honours of Scotland?

A. Badges for Bravery
B. A Music Band
C. Famous books
D. A Sword, Sceptre and Crown

22. When does Queen Elizabeth II stay at Holyrood Palace?

A. Winter
B. Summer
C. Spring
D. Autumn

23. When was the Union of Scotland and England?

A. 1788
B. 1801
C. 1707
D. 1777

24. What are Abbey Lairds?

A. Debtors
B. Scottish Dukes
C. Bishops of Holyrood
D. Lords of the Abbey

25. How much did the Scottish Parliament Building cost to build?

A. £10 million
B. £40 million
C. £50 million
D. £414 million

26. How much does the National Monument weigh?

A. 3 tonnes
B. 4 tonnes
C. 6 tonnes
D. 10 tonnes

For answers see next page...

LEFT St Stephens Church, Edinburgh

Design & Artwork: ALEX YOUNG

Published by: DEMAND MEDIA LIMITED

Publisher: JASON FENWICK

Written by: JANEY FLETCHER